Establishing Creative Writing Studies as an Academic Discipline

NEW WRITING VIEWPOINTS
Series Editor: Graeme Harper, *University of Wales, Bangor, Wales, Great Britain*

The overall aim of this series is to publish books which will ultimately inform teaching and research, but whose primary focus is on the analysis of creative writing practice and theory. There will also be books which deal directly with aspects of creative writing knowledge, with issues of genre, form and style, with the nature and experience of creativity, and with the learning of creative writing. They will all have in common a concern with excellence in application and in understanding, with creative writing practitioners and their work, and with informed analysis of creative writing as process as well as completed artefact.

Full details of all the books in this series and of all our other publications can be found on http://www.multilingual-matters.com, or by writing to Multilingual Matters, St Nicholas House, 31–34 High Street, Bristol, BS1 2AW, UK.

Establishing Creative Writing Studies as an Academic Discipline

Dianne Donnelly

MULTILINGUAL MATTERS
Bristol • Buffalo • Toronto

To Keith Gannon and Julia Page

Library of Congress Cataloging in Publication Data
A catalog record for this book is available from the Library of Congress.
Donnelly, Dianne.
Establishing Creative Writing Studies as an Academic Discipline/Dianne Donnelly.
New Writing Viewpoints: 7
Includes bibliographical references.
1. Creative writing–Study and teaching. I. Title.
PE1404.D659 2011
808'.0420711dc23 2011035424

British Library Cataloguing in Publication Data
A catalogue entry for this book is available from the British Library.

ISBN-13: 978-1-84769-590-1 (hbk)
ISBN-13: 978-1-84769-589-5 (pbk)

Multilingual Matters
UK: St Nicholas House, 31–34 High Street, Bristol, BS1 2AW, UK.
USA: UTP, 2250 Military Road, Tonawanda, NY 14150, USA.
Canada: UTP, 5201 Dufferin Street, North York, Ontario M3H 5T8, Canada.

Copyright © 2012 Dianne Donnelly.

All rights reserved. No part of this work may be reproduced in any form or by any means without permission in writing from the publisher.

The policy of Multilingual Matters/Channel View Publications is to use papers that are natural, renewable and recyclable products, made from wood grown in sustainable forests. In the manufacturing process of our books, and to further support our policy, preference is given to printers that have FSC and PEFC Chain of Custody certification. The FSC and/or PEFC logos will appear on those books where full certification has been granted to the printer concerned.

Typeset by The Charlesworth Group.

Contents

List of Figures vii
Acknowledgements viii

Introduction: The Emergence of *Creative Writing Studies*. 1
   The Disciplinary Status of Creative Writing/*Creative Writing Studies*   4
   The Emergence of *Creative Writing Studies* – Where to Begin? . . .   6
   Establishing *Creative Writing Studies* as an Academic Discipline . . 10

Section 1
A Taxonomy of Creative Writing Pedagogies. 15
   Where Meaning Lies – A Multi-Faceted Approach. 19
   Orientation of Critical Theories. 22
   The Objective Theory as New Criticism 24
   The Expressivist Theory 41
   The Mimetic Theory as Imitable Functions 56
   The Pragmatic Theory as Reader-Response. 60

Section 2
The Writing Workshop Model 73
   A Workshop Survey 74
   Defining the Workshop Model. 76
   A Study of the Workshop Model. 78
   How Our Workshop History Informs Our Praxes. 83
   Perceptions and Practice 89
   Developing Markers of Professional Difference 108
   The Case for Creative Writing Research as Knowledge 119
   The Workshop Model: Final Arguments. 126

Section 3
The Academic Home of *Creative Writing Studies* 131
    Control of Space, Domain and Power 133
    The Academic Home of *Creative Writing Studies* 134

Conclusion: The Legitimacy of *Creative Writing Studies* 148
References 152

List of Figures

Figure 1 Artistic communication transaction 23
Figure 2 Abrams's taxonomy of theories 23
Figure 3 Donnelly's taxonomy of theories 23

Acknowledgements

As writers, we read the world as text; and as writer-teachers, we share our recursive practices with our students and invest in and encourage their development as writers. As writer-scholars and researchers, we bring more meaning to the academy, its profession and its student body by establishing distinguishing features of our practice and implementing an intelligent and practical curricular design that includes the transfer of new skills to our creative writing students. As writers, writer-teachers, writer-scholars and researchers, we are able to add to the larger conversation of creative writing as an academic discipline because of the influence, collaboration and encouragement of others. With this in mind, the following are some of the people to whom I am very grateful:

- To Graeme Harper and Anna Roderick for their guidance and belief that this book would complement the many other voices in the *New Writing Viewpoints* series that inform creative writing teaching and research. To all of their wonderful staff for their attention to detail and gracious communication.
- To the teachers who contributed to my 2010 workshop survey and the many more who engaged in dynamic email exchanges with me. The pulse of creative writing bounds, in part, because of their input. In particular, I wish to thank Randall Albers, Nancy McCabe, Karl Elder, Lisa Roney, Toni Graham, Linda Spaar, Peter Harris, Martin Cockroft, Grant Matthew Jenkins, Mark Wallace, Monica Berlin, Lorna Jackson, Gaylene Perry, Robert Boswell, Keith Kumasin Abbott, Jane Hillberry, Janet McCann, Valerie Martinez, Judith Braumel, Karen Holmberg, Lorna Jackson, Deanna Kern Ludwin, Lex Runciman, Juliet Davis, Donald Platt, List Russ Spaar, McKeel McBride, Susan Carol Hauser,

John Meredith Hill, Gary Hawkins, Maurice Manning, Leslie Adrienne Miller, B.W. Jorgensen, Lisa Lewis, T.R. Hummer, Grant Matthew Jenkins, J. T. Bushnell, Thom Brucie, Peter Harris, Arielle Greenburg and Allison Cummings. I'm grateful to Stephen Tatum for his email exchanges and to Philip Gerard for taking the time to talk with me at the 2011 AWP conference.

- To the writer-teachers and writer-scholars and researchers who continue to add new knowledge to the field of creative writing through their scholarship and panel forums at national and international conferences.
- To my colleagues and friends Joe Moxley and Pat Bizzaro, for blazing trails, making discoveries and championing my work.
- To my colleagues Rita Ciresi, John Fleming and Hunt Hawkins.
- To my students who continue to galvanize our writing communities and renegotiate new writing spaces.
- To my children Keith Gannon and Julia Page, two wonderful human beings who are the source of my inspiration and courage.
- To my family and my friends, in particular, to Chris Donnelly (Mom) and Karen Steele (Sissy), who are inextricably to me, both family and friends.

Introduction: The Emergence of *Creative Writing Studies*

The field of creative writing stands once again at a crossroads. On one side of the road is a course of study, a 'discipline' that is unaware of the histories and theories that inform its practice. As such, its 'creative writing teachers are, of necessity, implicated in questions of theory and practice' (Bishop, 1992a). In fact, some have charged creative writing 'as the most untheorized, and in that respect, anachronistic area in the entire constellation of English studies' (Haake, 2000: 49). We need only look at its historical precedents to understand these intimations. On the other side of the road is *creative writing studies*, an emerging field of scholarly inquiry and research. As an academic discipline, it explores and challenges the pedagogy of creative writing.

It might be said that creative writing has stood at a crossroads many times in its history. Consider, for example, its years of promoting literature for its own sake until its intersection with post-war program expansion and rising enrollment. Patrons of university subsidies and National Endowment for the Arts (NEA) funding made hiring opportunities available that tripled what is available in today's job market. In the eighties, the road traveled by creative writing promoted the production of writers and teachers until the 1990s, when, once again, creative writing situated at a byroad – this new position no longer in sync with a favorable marketplace.

For most of its history, creative writing has been a field that avoids scholarship. It maintains – even today – the mysterious element of creativity and hires successful writers on the assumption that they make the best teachers. On the whole, creative writing relies on the tradition of the workshop model as its signature[1] pedagogy – although we are now beginning to see some new activities in the workshop space. Even though student numbers might suggest creative writing's equal status with other disciplines in English studies – and in spite of Allan Tate's projection that '[c]reative writing is here to stay, at least for a long time' (1964: 181) – the

1

discipline stands yet again at a crossroads. It does so, in part, because it is 'an academic anomaly' (Tate, 1964: 182), popular with undergraduates, in particular, but nonetheless, a discipline that does not follow the same research requirements (or research methodologies) of its neighboring disciplines in literary and composition studies. As a discipline, creative writing is part of a fractured community signaled by its long history of subordination to literary studies, its lack of status and sustaining lore, and its own resistance to reform. In the past, these factions had kept creative writing from achieving any central core in the academy.

Creative writing studies, on the other hand, not only supports but welcomes intellectual analyses that may reveal new theories. Such theories have important teaching implications and insights into the ways creative writers read, write and respond. In fact, as a necessary step in embracing its own identity and scholarship, *creative writing studies* considers its 'markers of professional difference' (Ritter, 2001: 208), those identifying features which distinguish its field from composition studies and literary studies. The discipline also explores creative writing research as knowledge, its practitioners appreciating that writing processes and research reveal new insights that add operational significance to the field. Finally, *creative writing studies* promotes the hiring of those writer-teachers who propel the field forward by means of scholarly production and pedagogical presentations.

Creative writing and *creative writing studies* are two distinct enterprises. Although both entities overlap in some ways, the primary differences between the two relate to inquiry and research. Whereas the curricular design of creative writing programs continues (and plans to continue) to offer value-added writing and reading strategies for students who want to develop their writing/reading skills and improve their works-in-progress, the ascending field of *creative writing studies* – as a separate program track – rethinks its pedagogy and scholarship and shifts its educational goals. Still in its nascent phase, *creative writing studies* must undergo necessary inquiries and research into its field in order to fully develop and be measured as an academic discipline. It must also establish markers of professional difference and training for its new teachers so as to carry on its inquiry and research and to teach new skills to its students. The academic goal of *creative writing studies* is to stand alongside composition studies and literary studies and any other university field of study as a separate-but-equal discipline.

This book argues for the ascendancy of *creative writing studies* as an academic discipline. Its study explores the history of creative writing, its workshop model as its primary practice, and the discipline's major pedagogical practices. Through its pedagogical and historical inquiry of the field, this argument is intended as a small contribution to the development of *creative writing studies*. Its research includes a workshop survey of undergraduate creative writing teachers, scholarship in the field and pedagogical practices that reveal new understandings. The argument envisions a more robust, variable and intelligent workshop model. It considers how an understanding of our pedagogical practices might influence our teaching strategies and classroom dynamics and how we might provide more meaning to the academy, our profession and our diverse student body.

At a curricular level, this book recommends course and program development that would meet the needs of creative writing students at all levels, and it justifies the importance of including graduate-level training for teacher preparation to further explore the field's history and pedagogy. The driving intent of this argument is to pilot *creative writing studies* into the future and to define its academic home.

The book is organized into three parts. The first explores the pedagogical practices in creative writing. Building on M.H. Abrams's 'triangle' of author, work and reader, I characterize the four major pedagogical theories in the creative writing classroom as New Critical, Expressive, Mimetic and Reader-Response. The various theories all concern where teachers privilege meaning in the composing process. As a part of the inquiry, historical antecedents that impact the discipline's practices – and in some cases, its isolationist posture in the English department – are explored along with the scope of teaching strategies and their implications. While I examine the historical antecedents and pedagogical practices of each theory, I find it useful to apply Lacanian theory as a means of comprehending the relationships between teachers and students and in understanding students' identities and their responses to writing instruction. My concern in this section is that teachers often fail to recognize the theories that underpin their practices or they resist altering the routine of their teaching instruction. Moreover, they might unintentionally confuse their students by practicing one pedagogical model in the classroom and using another teaching method to evaluate students' work and performance. What I propose then is a four-part taxonomy of pedagogical practices so that – as appropriate – teachers may reconsider or modify their strategies and be clearer to students as to their expectations.

With a goal to help *creative writing studies* ascend as an academic discipline, the second part of this argument explores the history and current practices of the workshop model. The *workshop*, now an interchangeable signifier for the practice of creative writing, is often cast negatively by critics who condemn its lack of rigor and intelligence. The function of the workshop model raises questions about its usefulness and about students' readiness, preparation and effort. My argument demonstrates that although the model continues to be creative writing's principal pedagogy, some teachers are in fact changing and expanding the shape of the model and collaborating with other disciplines to explore performative art, digital technology, film studies and other creative arts. This section outlines variable curricular and program designs at the undergraduate and graduate levels as an important part of creating opportunities for the teaching of new skills to creative writers. Additionally, the second section of this book advances *creative writing studies* as a distinct field through an identification of distinguishing markers in the ways creative writing students read, write and respond in the workshop practice.

My final section regards the academic home of *creative writing studies*, weighing such factors as the current marginalization of creative writing in the English department and the discipline's possible mergence with literary studies, cultural studies, composition studies or as one component in an independent writing program. In the end, I situate *creative writing studies* shoulder-to-shoulder with literary studies and composition studies as a pedagogically and programmatically sound entity fully empowered in its own identity and scholarship.

The Disciplinary Status of Creative Writing/*Creative Writing Studies*

I want to lay some basic groundwork in terms of defining what is meant when we talk about the teaching of creative writing as a profession and the legitimacy of *creative writing studies* as a discipline and as a field of study. While teaching is generally seen as a *form* of professional work, one that requires a great deal of specialized knowledge (Sykes *et al.,* 1985), the label 'profession' is thought to be reserved for establishments of long standing such as law, medicine and clergy. Other formations may develop and these are better known as 'occupations', which may aspire to be professions, but the initiation to reach this status is apparently long and arduous. There are educational policy references that address reformations for professionalizing teaching, but allegedly, as educators, we are not there yet – teaching is still an occupation. Still many of us refer to teaching as a 'profession'. Semantics and decades of general usage of the term 'profession' around college campuses and conferences give us some unofficial card-carrying right to refer to creative writing teaching as a profession, I suppose. However, what this unsanctioned posture amounts to is that the teaching of creative writing cannot be measured against any uniformed standard of profession.

As a discipline or field of study, creative writing can already claim status in the English department through its specialized academic programs, its professional organization, conferences and publications. Most importantly, it can be argued that creative writing is a growing professional body of knowledge, one which considers the acts and actions of writers. Creative writing's history is a hybrid of theories and practices drawn in part from composition studies and literary studies, of which creative writing's practice today is still mostly affected. Although creative writing has drawn epistemologically from this base, it continues to constitute practices that are independent of those in composition studies and literary studies, praxes that are guided by writerly and readerly processes of creative writers. In many ways then creative writing is a thriving field.

In other ways, though, the discipline falls short in terms of its graduate career training to include teacher preparation, its articulated research agenda and academic forums, and in ways in which its practitioners might claim it as a research area. Because creative writing practitioners are not well-informed regarding the history that informs their practices, it makes sense that there would be challenges to theorizing the principles that underpin their practices. Scholars often rebuke creative writing on the premise that it is not really a field of inquiry and research as writing is not often apprised as a research method. '[W]riting is usually regarded not as a research method, but as a means of presenting the results of research' (Cook, 2005: 198).

Professor Lee Shulman, President of the Carnegie Foundation for the Advancement of Teaching, tells us that the professions of law, medicine, engineering and the clergy have what he calls 'signature pedagogies' (2005b: 52), the salient, pervasive teaching practices that characterize a field. When we consider the teaching practices that categorize the field of law, we think of the Socratic-like questioning based on case studies, and in medicine, clinical rounds are a standard. Creative writing's signature pedagogy is the writing workshop, and the model – given its personal nature – functions as a hybrid of New Criticism, social-expressivism, Romanticism, mimesis and social cognitivism. This is important to mention because the signature pedagogy of a profession often reflects the stability of that profession. In brief, as a signature pedagogy, the traditional workshop model, without a more rigorous and intellectual focus, does not best represent the stability of creative writing as a discipline.

Shulman notes that there are both advantages and disadvantages associated with a field's signature pedagogy. These teaching practices are also 'subject to change as conditions in the practice of the profession itself and in the institutions that provide professional service or care undergo larger societal change' (2005b: 52). Shulman provides another caveat to consider, one which he refers to as 'pedagogical inertia' (2005a), an idleness that can occur when teaching practices are sustained within a field simply because those practices have been around for a very long time. A parallel might be made to Stephen North's (1987) concept of 'lore' and its sustainable influence on practices and behavior. While Schulman (and North) might very well be addressing creative writing's workshop model in this discussion of prolonged practices, there seems – inferential in his address – other functions that once investigated might reveal *creative writing studies'* potential for growth as an intellectual force. Bizzaro has long argued that 'a discipline is characterized by what it construes as proof of evidence.'[2] I suggest then that *creative writing studies* can present such 'proof of evidence' that will support the field as an academic discipline.

Creative writing studies is differentiated from creative writing by its emphasis on collecting, compiling and presenting data. This new research area with its depth of inquiry, research and scholarship will better define its professional body of knowledge in an even more useful way.

While history can shed insight into creative writing's classroom praxes, Bizzaro notes, 'The history of the moment must be on training the next generation of writing teachers while encouraging them at the same time to be writers.'[3] As a discipline centered on inquiry and research, *creative writing studies* is aligned with this 21st century goal.

The Emergence of *Creative Writing Studies* – Where to Begin?

As *creative writing studies* is still in its budding phase of development, the first step in its field of inquiry requires an exploration of the nature of its existing scholarship and research. Bizzaro contends that once creative writers have assessed what studies have been completed – once they have explored the nature of scholarship – they can then determine what remains to be completed in its field of inquiry. To be clear, efforts to establish *creative writing studies* as an academic discipline might include inquiries and research into the field's pedagogy and its history. Moreover, the advancement of *creative writing studies* in the academy depends on institutional advocacies to include the support of creative writing faculty as well as public advocacies that might reconsider the lore of creative writing and the merits of *creative writing studies* as an academic discipline.

Two examples of scholarship that explore creative writing's pedagogy include studies by Patrick Bizzaro and Kelly Ritter. Both inquire into current practices in an effort to establish epistemological differences and claims for academic development. Bizzaro and Ritter are explicit about the need to assert our distinctive methodology from other subjects in English studies so as to develop new theories and skill-sets, which creative writing teachers can then teach to their students through new course development. Ritter's (2001) inquiry into the training programs that best prepare graduate students for the teaching of creative writing presents interview and survey results in 'Professional Writers/Writing Professional: Revamping Teacher Training in Creative Writing Ph.D. Programs'. Bizzaro (2004) demonstrates research in creative writing by differentiating some of our disciplinary practices in 'Research and Reflection in English Studies: The Special Case of Creative Writing'. These published inquiries and research further advance what Tim Mayers (2009: 220) references, characteristically, as the pedagogical strand of *creative writing studies*.

Other scholarship that questions creative writing pedagogy and its relationship to English studies includes Joseph Moxley's (1989) collection *Creative Writing in America: Theory and Pedagogy*, Wendy Bishop's (1990) *Released Into Language: Options for Teaching Creative Writing*, Bishop and Hans Ostrom's (1994) collection *Colors of a Different Horse: Rethinking Creative Writing Theory and Pedagogy*, Patrick Bizzaro's (1993) *Responding to Student Poems*, the collections of Anna Leahy (2005) *Power and Identity in the Creative Writing Classroom: The Authority Project*, and Kelly Ritter and Stephanie Vanderslice's (2007) *Can It Really Be Taught?: Resisting Lore in Creative Writing Pedagogy*, Tim Mayers (2005) *(Re)Writing Craft: Composition, Creative Writing, and the Future of English Studies*, Katharine Haake's (2000) *What Our Speech Disrupts: Feminism and Creative Writing Studies* and Michelene Wandor's (2008) *The Author is Not Dead, Merely Somewhere Else: Creative Writing Reconceived*.

My edited collection *Does the Writing Workshop Still Work?* (2010) includes inquiries and studies of the workshop model as it relates to contact zones, hybrid models, epistemological differences, risks, vulnerabilities, conflicts, experimentation, spaces for radical openness, master classes and implications for our writers in the internet generation, among other topics. Moreover, there is a host of essays not included in this catalogue of scholarship that questions current practices and offers epistemological differences.

The titles alone in this well-developed pedagogical strand of inquiry announce the kind of critical studies that might stimulate further research. At the very least, such an inquiry into existing scholarship generates a sum of questions. For example, what can this strand of pedagogy tell us about creative writers' research methods and how they construct and construe data? How are these research methods different from other disciplines in English studies? What conclusions might be drawn in terms of other professional differences? In what ways does this breadth of scholarship reflect teaching practices and the methods by which creative writing students read and write? In what venues will creative writers publish their findings, present their questions and/or compare their modes of instruction?

As it relates to programmatic changes, we might ask creative writing teachers to consider if and/or how their course development passes new skills on to their students. As it is critical to make important changes that reflect the unique nature of research and pedagogy in creative writing's current curriculum, we could question how we might re-envision and revise existing coursework. Bizzaro (2004: 308), specifically, refers to courses that are often taught by non-specialists in the English department such as 'Bibliography and Methods of Literature Research', and 'Literature: the Writer's Perspective'. These courses should be designed to reflect creative writing's specificity, its own bibliographies, and they must be taught with creative writers in mind.

In addition to the pedagogical segments of *creative writing studies*, Mayers includes institutional and theoretical historical strands as areas of inquiry, scholarship and research. While D.G. Myers (1996) presents a macrocosmic overview of creative writing's history in *The Elephant's Teach* – managing as well, Mayers (2009: 222) tells us, 'to produce a foundational work in creative writing studies' – we should look to other work and approaches as we take into account this institutional substrand. We might, for example, consider creative writing's institutional history in a new light as it speculates the ways in which composition and literary theories have informed our pedagogy and how this information leads to new understandings for the field of *creative writing studies*. Along the same lines, there is value in studying the polarization of creative writing and literary studies to reconstitute this history as an opportunity for exerting our presence and space in the emerging field of *creative writing studies*. Moreover, in surveying the major creative writing pedagogical practices we might merge theory, inquiry and practice in new ways by applying Lacanian theory to reveal how teacher-student relationships might be viewed in the context of our pedagogical choices.

Advocacy within the institution is critical to the success of our emerging enterprise. I give evidence of ways in which creative writing has 'exhibited a powerful isolationist tendency, while existing nominally within

English departments' (Mayers, 2009: 224). To reverse this marginalization (no one can erase the history of creative writing's peripheral status) means positioning creative writers in a more visible and comfortable academic home. This situating requires an institutional advocacy measure that 'would focus on examining and arguing for the proper place of creative writing and creative writers within existing academic structures' (Mayers, 2009: 224). To add to this dialogue, there are opportunities to rethink program development to better prepare creative writing students at variable degree and program levels. With this in mind, I outline specific options for creative writing and *creative writing studies* at the undergraduate, MFA and PhD levels.

Also at the academic advocacy level, Mayers (2009: 225) offers opportunities for scholars in *creative writing studies* to intersect with compositionists as a means of 'explor[ing] the implications of new electronic forms of text distribution'. Beyond this intersection, we witness the forward movement of *creative writing studies* as creative writing teachers embrace and incorporate more technological literacy skills (literary hypertext, digital narratives, podcasts and such) into their course design. While we witness a decline in printed books and material (and appreciate that a symbiotic relationship exists between the printed and digital text), we see creativity and technology merge in ways that (1) transcend academic disciplines and the digital culture of universities and (2) consider – for our students as creative artists in the 21st century – new audiences, relative skills and practical opportunities in writing in digital environments. Many more collaboration possibilities exist for *creative writing studies* in the field of media design, the fine arts and the creative industries – areas I discuss at further length. In fact, creative writing courses – particularly when they include multimodal literacies and disciplinary collaboration – provide value-added relevance as a core requirement of the college curriculum. Two decades ago, Wendy Bishop suggested the creative writing course as a general education requirement, and while creative writing enrollment has continued to increase (despite naysayers' claims that these numbers should plateau) – department heads and university administrators question the financial feasibility of such a requirement given the relatively small class size of creative writing courses compared with the class size of many university-based course offerings. However, renewed interest in creative writing as a foundational course appears on the rise as evidenced by 2011 AWP (Association of Writers & Writing Programs) conference sessions where panelists energized the claim that creative writing can enhance the outcomes embedded in the university's core curriculum.

Finally, the public lore of creative writing (to include the popular images of the writer and the writing process) surrounds and impacts the credibility and effectiveness of creative writing as an academic discipline, and thus *creative writing studies* as a scholarly discipline. Investigating the field of lore compels not only inquiries and research in this area but intensive public advocacy and scholarship written with a more general audience in mind. Kelly Ritter and Stephanie Vanderslice (2007), along with contributors in their edited collection *Can It Really Be Taught?: Resisting Lore in Creative Writing Pedagogy*, have begun such an inquiry, and I continue this conversation in my workshop scholarship. To diminish such lore would require not only a considerable community shift in the perception and promotion of creative writing but also substantial institutional buy-in. The acceptance of the emergence of *creative writing studies* depends on these advocacies.

Establishing *Creative Writing Studies* as an Academic Discipline

As a developing field of inquiry, scholarship and research, *creative writing studies* can bring more meaning to the academy, its profession and its student body as it establishes distinguishing features of its practice and implements a more intelligent and practical curricular design that includes the transfer of new skills to our creative writing students. Many questions remain as we proceed: What will our students draw from our classes? How will administrators view our developments? In what other ways might we claim our own identity through scholarship? As *creative writing studies* continues its valid inquiries into its practice and more formally establishes its body of professional knowledge, its goals, and its best direction, it does so with the farsightedness of a larger project of demystifying its process and reconfiguring not only the restructure of English studies but its contribution to the academy.

Creative writing studies can participate in such a restructure, sophisticated in its understanding that the various disciplines within the English department have been rivals at times, partners at times. As the new discipline emerges, it does so with intentions to intersect and commingle with other disciplines, other departments, even community services. As the discipline matures and can refer to evidence of its own research methodology and collective data, *creative writing studies* will stand on equal ground with literary studies and composition studies because its academic degrees will be conferred upon *academically-trained* candidates, because its rigorous programs exist *within* the academy, and because it can *locate* its authority in its *own* scholarship.

My argument explores the pedagogical problems of the discipline, researches the field's history and teaching practices, and defines and distinguishes critical landmarks to differentiate the discipline from others. As a study of inquiry and research, this scholarship attempts to advance *creative writing studies* as an academic discipline.

Notes

1. Lee Shulman references signature pedagogies in his essay 'Signature Pedagogies in the Professions', and Anna Leahy links Shulman's awareness of 'signature' pedagogies to creative writing's workshop pedagogy in 'Teaching as a creative act: Why the workshop works in creative writing'. In D. Donnelly (ed.) *Does the Writing Workshop Still Work?* (pp. 63–77). Bristol: Multilingual Matters.
2. This comment results from my email communications with Patrick Bizzaro. I want to note my appreciation of these dynamic and resourceful communications on the subject of *creative writing studies* – its history, its present state of affairs and its future.
3. Ibid

SECTION 1

A Taxonomy of Creative Writing Pedagogies

Where Meaning Lies – A Multi-Faceted Approach

Orientation of Critical Theories

The Objective Theory as New Criticism

The Expressivist Theory

The Mimetic Theory as Imitable Functions

The Pragmatic Theory as Reader-Response

A Taxonomy of Creative Writing Pedagogies

While the field of composition studies yields many useful taxonomies and axiologies on the teaching of writing, the field of *creative writing studies* is just beginning to emerge in this area of research. Composition's cognitive approaches, in particular, which sought correspondence between writing and learning and between how writers make decisions and choices in the writing process, might have served as a platform for parallel research in creative writing practice. It might have bridged a discussion from the writing and learning practices of creative writers to the ways in which we privilege certain teaching approaches and how these practices inform course planning, teaching strategies and classroom structure. Likewise, the field of literary studies has concerned itself with the research and study of literature from multiple (albeit conflicting) perspectives, presenting for creative writing, at a minimum, alternative methodologies for perceiving a text as verbal icon and for challenging master narratives.

What I discover when I survey the creative writing landscape for studies in teaching theories is limited. This is in spite of Bishop's (1994) plea for creative writing research methodology, ethnographic studies and teacher self-reports and Moxley's (1989) proposal for the interrogation of creative writing practices. Their work, often cited in today's scholarship, has moved the field forward only incrementally, perhaps because, as Moxley notes, creative writing teachers have a 'relative lack of interest in pedagogy' (1989: 27). Creative writing's isolationist posture is 'centuries old', and this stultifying stance leads Bizzaro to conclude that creative writers are skeptical 'of anything academic' (2004: 296). A mirroring of this 'view of science-as-devourer [is] put forth perhaps most emphatically and influentially in America by Edgar Allan Poe' in his 'In Sonnet – To Science': 'Why preyest thou thus upon the poet's heart, / Vulture, whose wings are dull realities?' (qtd. in Bizzaro, 2004: 296).

In general, creative writers and writer-teachers seem to talk *around* the subject of research. The discipline often does not produce outcome data. It has little tangible evidence that affirms that our teaching methods improve student writing. In fact, because creative writing has often been defined by its writing workshop model, some in the field wonder if there is a substantial discipline from which to draw data on its teaching theories and practices, and if so, Shirley Geok-lin Lim (2003: 151) questions, 'How should we begin to talk about such a discipline?'

It may come as no surprise that creative writing lags in the study and theorizing of its teaching practices when we appreciate that the majority of graduate creative writing programs do not include coursework related to the pedagogy of creative writing, and only a handful of such programs provides training in teacher preparation. Ritter (2001: 213), who surveyed PhD creative writing programs in 2001, concludes, '[m]ost U.S. universities have no specific training in place that would prepare candidates to enter the creative writing classroom even remotely as well prepared as their rhetoric and composition Ph.D. counterparts'. The point to be made here is twofold: The first is that teacher training should assuredly include topics and/or courses in the history of creative writing, the theories behind pedagogical approaches, research methodologies in creative writing, contemporary issues in creative writing and, possibly, curricular design. The second reason to champion teacher training is partly rolled into the first point in that an awareness of historical approaches should lay the groundwork for important research studies that influence how we practice, how we teach our students and where meaning lies in our classrooms. It stands to reason that an immersion in the field's history and in teacher training will lead to more critical rethinking of our modes of instruction as well as notions on how this critical rethinking will translate to *what* and *how* we teach our students.

Mayers calls for an inquiry into the field's history beyond the contextualization of creative writing. There exist a few important historical inquires such as D.G. Myers's (1996) *The Elephants Teach*, Stephen Wilbers's (1980) *The Iowa Writers Workshop*, Patrick Bizzaro's (1993) *Responding to Student Poems* and Paul Dawson's (2005) *Creative Writing and the New Humanities*. Of the books mentioned, only Bizzaro and Dawson directly suggest ways to learn from creative writing's history and offer new avenues to approach its practice. What Mayers has in mind when he calls his fellow craft critics to action is for creative writing teachers to go beyond this historical research to discover different ways to consider our history, to explore new paths to contextualize its meaning and to construct variable lenses from which to view history in a different light. I suggest that there is still much we can learn from the history of creative writing from Emerson's naming of creative writing in his 1837 essay 'The American Scholar' to contemporary creative writing praxes in university programs that might better inform our pedagogy. There exists significant data *from* which we can draw conclusions related to our teaching approaches and *by* which we might better integrate strategic program development in light of the new challenges we face in the 21st century.

In the early nineties, Bishop laments that creative writing teachers know little of the theory that informed their pedagogies and, as such, they could not voice the tenets behind their classroom practices because they lack reference. Almost a decade later, D.W. Fenza (2000) advances this same concern when he says, '[f]ew writers in the academy know the history of their own profession as teachers of writing'. In fact, Bizzaro (2004: 295) suggests practitioners 'view creative writing as something that has stumbled, by chance alone, into academe'. What is more, because writers do not know their history, they miss opportunities to address the theoretical rationale of the practices in their classroom. As such, Fenza tells us that 'they sometimes find it hard to defend their work against the scholars, the theorists and commentators who trivialize it'. If we are to bring the relevancy of history to current teaching practices, then we must include the view of English department chairs such as Stephen Tatum, the 1993 department chair at the University of Utah, whose essay in the *ADE Bulletin* forewarns 'The end of creative writing in the English department'. While Tatum's discussion does not necessarily include the teaching of creative writing, he does regret the curricula of graduate programs, which position the history of genres and of literature as an adversary to the creative writing candidate. His complaint has significance for the creative writing graduate who interviews for tenure-track positions today. This lack of history and it pertinence to a candidate's field and subsequently to her teaching opportunities is a reality we cannot ignore or resist in our reform. Given creative writing's changing goals, those which move us from a generation of publishing writers to a generation of teachers performing in the creative industries of education and business, it is time, as Bizzaro (2004: 300) urges, 'to reconsider the way we think of creative writing as a teachable subject'.

It becomes difficult, I suggest, to ground theoretical underpinnings to our teaching pedagogy without such historical reference. Moreover, the lack of empirical data and investigative studies into creative writing's teaching praxes leaves much of what goes on in the creative writing classroom unexamined, untheorized. Consequently, creative writing continues to operate from a base of assumptions that is situated more on practice than on research. However, if creative writing practitioners can agree on the principle that *what* they teach in their creative writing classes filters down to *how* they teach their creative writing students, then it is possible to break this hypothesis down further to conclude that methods of pedagogy are driven by a teacher's perception of *where meaning lies* in the context of the writing process. What a teacher privileges as it relates to text, writer, reader and reality (as an implicit or explicit world-view) is tied directly to her pedagogies, to the structure of her classroom, to her course planning, selection of readings, choice of exercises and assignments, reading practices, classroom management, workshop practice, social relations – and evaluation, justification and the grading of course requirements.

As my research interest relies on history, pedagogical implications and curricular design, what I propose is a four-part taxonomy of teaching approaches that converge, in part, on the principles underlying James Berlin's (1982: 765) analysis of teaching differences as those 'located in the diverging definitions of the composing process itself'. Berlin insists that all pedagogy is ideological; any single approach supports an underlying set of values while questioning others. These rhetorical elements are often represented as a triangle and, as such, the element placed within the triangle assumes the greatest teacher emphasis. Pedagogy, as John Trimbur reminds us, is exacted by ideology.

Similarly, the operational pedagogy of creative writing teachers can be analyzed according to a set of interactions among the elements of the composing process. Equivalently, teaching differences of creative writing teachers are located as disparate *privileging* (rather than *definitions*) of the composing process.

While Berlin (1982: 766) identifies four principal pedagogical theories and concerns each with the way it interprets and associates writer, reality, audience and language 'to form a distinct world construct with distinct rules for discovering and communicating knowledge', his classifications and purposes do not necessarily align optimally for the case of creative writing pedagogy. The dominant composition teaching theories engage with, among other elements, principles of truth and its relationship with the world and to language, reality as it exists to the writer and inductive versus deductive processes.

This is an oversimplification, of course, of the field's teaching constructs; however, there is more relevance in an analysis of creative writing's salient pedagogies and their strategies for communicating where meaning lies in the composing processes in M.H. Abrams's (1953) four overriding theories of artistic transaction as outlined in *The Mirror and the Lamp*. I approach my taxonomy of creative writing pedagogies by using Abrams's classifications to explain his: (1) objective theory – which describes New Criticism, a creative writing pedagogy that privileges meaning with the text, (2) expressivist theory – to detail *expressivist functions of self-expression* as well as the influences of Romanticism, both which place meaning for the creative writing teacher with the writer, (3) mimetic theory – to discuss the *imitable functions* of the writer's world that emphasize that meaning lies with the 'universe', and (4) pragmatic theory – to characterize *reader-response pedagogy* that situates meaning with the reader.

Moreover, a second major strand in an axiological study of teaching practices involves the complicated social relations within the structure of our creative writing classrooms that are created, in part, by the constructs of our methods and philosophies. As practitioners, we tend to oversimplify the interactive and dialectical nature of the teacher-student relationship. However, when teachers can view their classroom dynamics through a Lacanian lens, they can better understand the actualities of students' behavior both in class and in their writing and how teacher-student interaction influences such behavior. More specifically, psychoanalytic theory offers valuable and concrete assistance in explaining – through Lacanian theories of the Real, Imaginary, and Symbolic orders and the dynamics of transference and counter-transference – what goes on beneath the surface of our writing instruction and how we might decode it more constructively for ourselves and for our students.

Where Meaning Lies – A Multi-Faceted Approach

In *Professing Literature: An Institutional History*, Gerald Graff (1987: 10) contends that 'no text is an island'. Todd F. Davis and Kenneth Womack (2002: 1) add that 'no form of theory or act of criticism is an island either'. Graeme Harper (2006: 1) cautions us not to moor our students' learning to one specific island when he suggests in his introduction to *Teaching Creative Writing* that the 'learning of creative writing' by our students 'gains nothing at all from being considered the remit of only one type of learner or one type of teacher'. Richard Fulkerson (1990: 424) offers that '[e]ven if you know where you want to go, a shrewd Cheshire Cat can point out more than one path to get you there, as well as some attractive ones that won't'. Moreover – and this is an axiom borrowed from James Berlin's (1982: 766) taxonomy of composition pedagogical approaches – creative writing teachers must also be cognizant that through their determinable intent, they 'are tacitly teaching a version of reality and the student's place and mode of operation in it'.

My posture leans more toward *not* privileging any one element of the communication transaction whether it is finding meaning with the text, the writer *or* the reader. Instead of a singular pedagogical focus, I believe we must continue to challenge and question the underlying set of values Berlin associates with each pedagogy so as to acknowledge the assorted and changing ideological forces at work. Teachers can avoid giving conflicting messages to their students when they are aware of their own pedagogies, stay current with research and scholarship, and make adjustments along the way to their approaches. Assessing our own pedagogy is critical to *what* and *how* we pass on writerly and readerly skills to our students. While there is expected overlap as Abrams suggests – 'Although any reasonably adequate theory takes some account of all four elements, almost all theories ... exhibit a discernible orientation toward one only' (p. 6) – teachers should be conscious of their pedagogical theories as much as this is possible.

Perhaps, it is even time for creative writing teachers to ask what alternative methods they might conceive in their classrooms. For example, creative writing teachers might begin with practices based in composition theory or literary studies theory and find new ways to apply such principles to the specifics of creative writing as they keep in mind the unique ways that creative writers think, read and write. Katherine Haake (1994: 81) concurs that there is value in engaging in a 'spirit of interdisciplinary curiosity' as it 'will help us reconstruct our own projects [pedagogies] in such a way as to respond not only to the needs of all our students but also to our own'. Stagnated as we may be on any one given practice – or worse – not knowing the implications of our practices, limits the direction of our teaching strategies, our course design and our students' ability to broaden their knowledge and reading/writing skills. We must, as Haake notes, 'reject as our purpose the unexamined, single-minded pursuit of the literary artifact', and once we can move beyond the kind of funneled teaching that contains us, we 'must then ask how we might begin to re-envision and transform not just our expectations of our students and their work, but those also of ourselves and our own work, at least within the context of our discipline' (1994: 81). Such re-envisioning and transforming might include varying classroom methodology, experimenting with different approaches and opening the creative writing course to the emergence of new theories that might come about as a result of the conscious blurring of lines between approaches. Studies and practices such as these propel *creative writing studies* forward as a separate and distinct discipline with research and scholarship of its own making.

As methods of pedagogy are driven by how we locate meaning in a text, one concern relates to model confusion, a case where teachers apply meaning in one composing structure but evaluate according to another. Our reading and writing processes are informed over years of practice and, as such, when we teach these processes to our students, we must be careful of conflicting theories. Bishop (1990: 15) cautions teachers that 'it is possible to hold unexamined or conflicting theories and to be resistant to theoretical and practical changes'. Too often teachers confuse their students when they apply differing motivating philosophies in the classroom. One approach may signify meaning in some element of practice (e.g. the reading of professional texts, the choice of writing prompts) and another as it relates to the evaluation emphasis (e.g. revision suggestions for student drafts, judgments of what constitutes 'good writing'). When our 'guidance [is] grounded in assumptions that simply do not square with each other' (Berlin, 1982: 766), we confound our students' learning.

Model confusion comes about when teachers are unaware of their practices. Sharon Crowley shares why the teacher who is either not cognizant of her practices or does not examine her pedagogy will tend to bewilder or mislead her students. Crowley hypothesizes how this might occur by noting that 'if a practitioner accepts recent lore concerning "process pedagogy", but has not altogether rejected traditional composition theory, it will be difficult for [her] to discern whether [her] particular combination of the two pedagogies entails contradictions or confusions' (qtd. in Bishop, 1990: 15). Bishop complicates this practice when she adds that '[n]ot only may a teacher implement conflicting pedagogical practices, she may overapply a model, which leads to classroom conditions that are just as restrictive as the ones she has abandoned' (1990: 15).

My aim in this four-part perspective is to deliver a clear and comprehensible view of what goes on in the creative writing classroom. This taxonomy of the four major creative writing pedagogies will help teachers examine and *name* their pedagogical practices and to root their methods and philosophies in one or more of the four pedagogies. I trace the historical antecedents of the four major teaching theories and demonstrate their current classroom practice, and, in each case, I outline the location of the teacher's authority in the composing process and the implications of such privilege. As a result, this study helps practitioners become aware of their pedagogies *and* the theories that underpin these practices. Such scholarship helps teachers present clearer writing processes to their students and adds to the kind of research necessary to establish the emergence of *creative writing studies* as an academic discipline.

Ideologically-based methods, values and emphases influence current approaches to the evaluation of student writing. We must continue to examine these approaches. Whenever possible, creative writing teachers should be aware of how their history enlightens their pedagogy. They can define their practice and be aware of where they place meaning in the communication transaction and how their privileging affects their pedagogy and their students. It is important also to consider teacher-student relations in the creative writing classroom, and – as such – perhaps a Lacanian perspective would be helpful.

At the very least, instructors can extend their pedagogical understandings by, as Gerald Graff (1995: 227) suggests, 'teaching the conflicts' in their courses, sharing with students how the shapes of their pedagogies are influenced by where they privilege meaning in the composing process, and in this dialogue they should aim for clarity in terms of what they consider and regard in their evaluative processes. My worry is that too many of us will become numb to the repetition in the organizing principles of our classroom, and if I can play with the pronouns of Katherine Haake's (2005: 99) words in 'Dismantling authority: Teaching what we do not know', I would ask: How many of us 'hear [ourselves] tell the same stories, say the same things – to teach, as it were, what [we] already knew?'. Later, Haake (2007: 5) speculates that 'perhaps it is time to acknowledge that there is no longer any one way in creative writing teaching, and to begin to ask what are the many ways there are?'. This taxonomy begins such a dialogue.

Orientation of Critical Theories

The nature and value of a work of art, the work's relationship to other variables (the writer, the audience, the universe), and the work as an autonomous whole constitute, for Abrams, the principal categories for defining, classifying and analyzing a work of art, as well as the major criteria by which the value of a work is judged. Like Berlin, Abrams's framework is best represented by a triangle. Unlike Berlin, who opens the triangle's center space for insertion of the element which receives the greatest emphasis, Abrams fixes the work of art as 'the thing to be explained' (1953: 6) in the center of his triangle. The relationship of the work to the artist, audience and universe is indicated by directional arrows as noted below (Figure 1).

Abrams is careful to observe that the four elements, which he defines as 'the total situation of a work of art' (p. 6), vary 'according to the theory in which they occur' (p. 7). For the purpose of my analysis, the centrality of the work of art in Abrams's framework is seen in more fluid or positional terms as are the remaining composing elements. The important schema is the teacher's motivational philosophy to any of the core composing processes: the work, the writer, the reader or the universe – or in the language of Abrams's corresponding pedagogical theories: the Objective, the Expressive, the Mimetic and the Pragmatic. In my theoretical framework, I refer

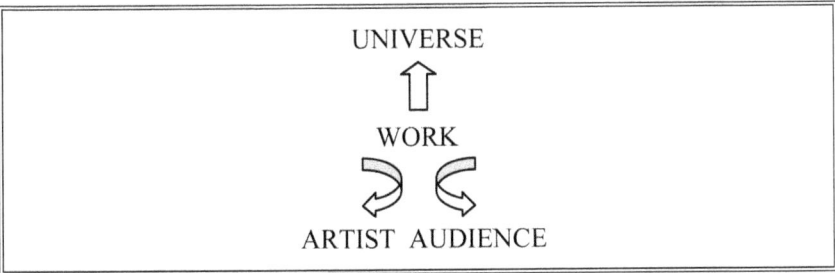

Figure 1 Artistic communication transaction

to Abrams's Objective Theory as New Criticism. I maintain his Expressive Theory terminology, but I split this theory into two strands: Self-Expressive and Romantic. The Mimetic Theory in the creative writing classroom remains predominantly the same as in Abrams's application although I also refer to it as an Imitable Theory. I get a bit more specific with Abrams's Pragmatic Theory and rename it Reader-Response Theory. The diagrams for Abrams's taxonomy of theories (Figure 2) and my taxonomy of theories (Figure 3) are shown below:

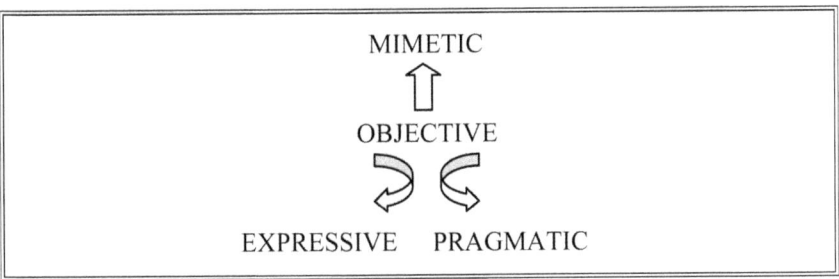

Figure 2 Abrams's taxonomy of theories

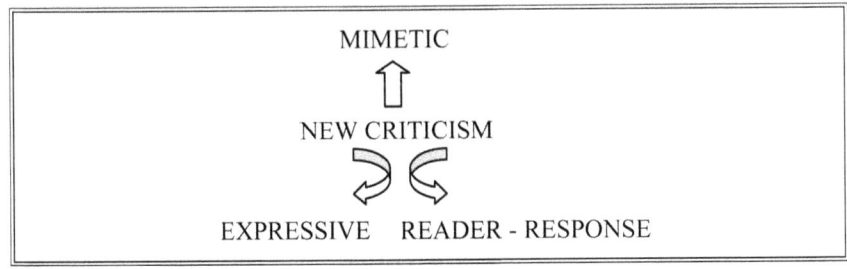

Figure 3 Donnelly's taxonomy of theories

The Objective Theory as New Criticism

Historical Antecedents

New Criticism functioned as a departure from the historical study of literature in the early 1920s to one in which the formalist characteristics and study of literature would be viewed from a technical standpoint. The passage of poet-critics into academia during the 1920s and 1930s coincided with, and was in part facilitated by, this practical criticism. The criticism for these young poet-critics grew out of their practical interest in writing poetry. In fact, it was through the tenets of the texts and the critical ways of reading by poets working as critics that soon advanced New Criticism as the dominant literary ideology. The key figure in this theory was T.S. Eliot, whose performance as critic and poet so impressed the academy that it was possible for poetry to be thought of as a 'wholly respectable undertaking' (Weiss, 1989: 152). This, in turn, helped to shape the American poets who came onto the academic scene in the 1940s, among them Robert Lowell, Elizabeth Bishop, John Berryman and Randall Jarrell (Myers, 1996: 129), the latter who claims no other age has 'so much extraordinarily good criticism of poetry'. The new critical approach to poetry during this period was said to have literally 'swept the country' (Weiss, 1989: 152).

Once creative writing became 'an institutional site for the literary authority of writers' (Dawson, 2005: 76), the practice of the workshop (which includes the close reading of student manuscripts) became situated and grounded on the principles of practical criticism, and creative writing concerned itself with analytical and evaluative perspectives of the text as a finished product. Between World War II and the term of the Vietnam Era, New Criticism mobilized as a means for teachers to remain apolitical in the university system. Bizzaro (1993) explains:

> [W]ell known is the theory that in the post World War II period, when university professors were anxious about having their political preferences called into question, the New Criticism, by virtue of its elevation of the text as authority for meaning, made the study of literature apolitical and, as a result, safer than innocent membership in certain social clubs. (p. 236)

In addition to wartime civics sustaining New Criticism as a measure of political privacy, Bizzaro concludes that the number of 'literary specialist' graduates over the 40-year span between World War II and the Vietnam Era led to the teaching of New Criticism in the academy (1993: 236). As such, it is not surprising that New Critical pedagogy and its privileging of the text persists as a major theoretical strand in our creative writing classrooms.

We know that once New Criticism became established in the university, its practitioners turned their scrutiny onto the internal structure of poems, applying the technique of close reading as a pedagogical tool. In this manner, New Criticism is linked to creative writing in that 'it devised an operational pedagogy – practical criticism – to promote its views of literature' (Dawson, 2005: 76). The New Critics did more than anyone to advance the cult of autonomy: the privileging of texts as verbal icons. Consider first, the widespread promulgation of *Understanding Poetry* (1938) as the quintessential textbook, and secondly – as an attachment to the book – a 'Letter to the Teacher' by which Cleanth Brooks and Robert Penn Warren clarified: 'though one may consider a poem as an instance of historical and ethical documentation, the poem in itself, if literature is to be studied as literature, remains finally the object of study' (qtd. in Myers, 1996: 130). Despite the fact that many say New Criticism is no longer a viable approach to the study of literature, it remains steadfast over the sovereignty of the poem (and story) so that it prevails more unflinchingly in the creative writing classroom than anywhere else. Here, it not only 'survives and is prospering', as a pedagogical practice, but it also 'seems to be powerless only because its power is so pervasive that we are ordinarily not even aware of it' (Cain, 1982: 1101).

Pedagogical Practice

Some, like Jane Thomkins, suggest that we have not renounced New Critical methods of reading and evaluating as these are the principles that 'everyone still carries around in their heads, whether they've been studying post-structuralism for twenty years or have only begun to study it today' (qtd. in Bizzaro, 1993: 39). As such, the ways in which we respond to texts are still linked, still 'tied to New Criticism's concern for unity and intensity of words-on-the-page' (Tilly Warnock, qtd. in Bizzaro, 1993: 39).

We can pick up the stitches of New Criticism initiated by the early 20th century partisans of criticism and locate their tight weave in the fabric of today's creative writing pedagogy. In particular, the practice of privileging texts as verbal icons, the ease of teaching from a New Critical perspective, and the standards of evaluation – its interpretation of the text as finished product, the teacher as exemplary reader and the issue of appropriation and text manipulation alone – are components of both interest and concern.

Texts as verbal icons

The teacher who places authority on the 'text' regards the work in isolation from any external reference. She 'analyzes it as a self-sufficient entity constituted by its parts in their internal relations, and sets out to judge it solely by criteria intrinsic to its own mode of being' (Abrams, 1953: 26). Her teaching strategies extend to an objective orientation, which affect all aspects of her teaching practice. In the creative writing classroom, where the object of criticism is the text, many teachers still depend on New Critical methods as a dominant pedagogy. Francine Prose (2006), in her book entitled *Reading Like a Writer*, shares the ways in which she learned to write. Her process and lessons for new writers echo New Critical ideology in that she offers how she reads 'more analytically, conscious of style, of diction, of how sentences were formed and information was being conveyed, how the writer was structuring a plot, creating characters, employing detail and dialogue' (p. 6). These elements, in their most basic forms, are the analytical and technical functions of a New Critical approach to a text. Prose suggests that '[a] good teacher can show [students] how to edit [their] work, how to appreciate' as she does, 'that writing, like reading, was done one word at a time, one punctuation mark at a time ... "putting every word on trial for its life"': changing an adjective, cutting a phrase, removing a comma, and putting the comma back in' (p. 3). Following the tenets of New Criticism, Prose states she 'read closely, word by word, sentence by sentence, pondering each deceptively minor decision the writer has made', in her unpacking of the story. In this method, students read published stories and their peers' work, scouting for elements of craft, tracing patterns, cracking codes, beginning, as many of us do, as close readers. As the practice of writing is often informed by reading, the focus on the elements of craft, what Jon Cook (2005: 199) may interpret as the 'routines of writing', might move the writer from craft to technique only when the writer discovers through her writing process and reflection something that takes her writing beyond the confines of a prescriptive New Criticism methodology. As an 'imperative requirement of method – "do this and this will result"', the learning of poetic forms and/or the stylistic manipulation of certain literary skills – what we know as craft – 'seems to be only weakly met' (Cook, 2005: 202) and can only be 'transformed into technique in a moment of discovery' (Seamus Heaney qtd. in Cook, 2005: 199). The tenets of New Criticism typically do not encourage such discovery as an important creative writing method.

Once creative writing became an institutional site for the literary authority of writers, the practice of the workshop as the field's fundamental pedagogy became situated and grounded on the principles of practical criticism, and the discipline concerned itself with analytical and evaluative perspectives of the text as a finished product. Ostrom (1994) recognizes the New Critical perspective in the workshop setting and teacher materials. He suggests, this objective theory persists today 'to a large extent' as 'it still dictates the terminology – and the view of the text as verbal icon – in workshops, anthologies, reviews and books on writing' (p. xv). The practice of New Critics 'to examine a poem' as a means of 'examin[ing] its construction – with the ruthless skepticism of someone who might have constructed it differently' (Ostrom, 1994: xv) is not unlike craft-based pedagogy, a practice of reading stories for the models of craft present in today's creative writing courses.

Because of its focus on craft elements, on what Ostrom refers to as 'durable Aristotelian aesthetic ideas' (p. xv), New Critical methods can often lead, in the workshopping of student texts, to an editorial orientation directed at technique and, as a result, issues that go beyond the text as an isolated object are not addressed as students are to read only the words on the page. Mayers (2005: 144) reiterates the influence of '[t]he technique-oriented Iowa workshop model', which he stipulates worked well for many students in terms of 'helping them toward revisions that enabled them to publish their creative work and, in some cases, helping them earn credentials that landed them jobs as professors of creative writing'. The latter, of course, perpetuated the recycling of New Critical pedagogical methods.

In fact, Mark McGurl (2007) suggests that the influence of New Criticism is evident in all of Flannery O'Connor's published work. O'Connor had attended the Iowa Workshop for two years. She studied with Robert Penn Warren, whose textbook/anthology that he co-authored with Cleanth Brooks, was publicly endorsed by O'Connor as her 'bible'. Eileen Pollack (2007: 547), another Iowa Workshop graduate, speaks generally of the New Critical approach as being 'in the air' at the Iowa Workshop. As it relates to O'Connor, Pollack claims 'the tenets of the New Criticism shows itself in the care with which she selects and arranges every concrete detail, every bit of dialogue, every gesture and larger action, whether to render the setting authentic or a character believable'. In fact, Pollack points to the specificity of O'Connor's New Critic detail as she 'gave the Misfit [in 'A Good Man is Hard to Find'] a black hat because that is what a man of his age and station would wear' (p. 552). Pollack and Mayers both echo my position that New Critical approaches in the creative writing classroom need to be identified as such; then re-evaluated as useful pedagogical tools – not to be used exclusively but rather, among the many approaches we offer to students.

To further illustrate the extent of the New Critic method in creative writing classrooms, Hal Blythe and Charlie Sweet (2008) define 'the techniques approach' (not meant to be confused with the transformation of craft to *technique* that Jon Cook and Seamus Heaney align with *discovery*) in their characterization of variable teaching strategies in creative writing classrooms. The authors include a 1913 definition of this method by Columbia professor George Krapp as a 'tendency on the part of some college instructors to place a great stress on the teaching of practical technique in literature' (qtd. in Blythe & Sweet, 2008: 312). This 'techniques approach' sounds very much like the New Critical practice of emphasizing inherent qualities in writing as a literal practice and pedagogical tool. Blythe and Sweet add to this description, noting the approach is one which emphasizes the illustration of technical components in readings so that students might internalize the technique and then offer their own version. 'The underlying belief of this approach', the authors write, 'is that the proper understanding of and practice with poetic, dramatic, creative nonfiction, and fictional techniques produce the works' (p. 313). While the technique in its 'practicality' can 'demystify' writing with its appeal 'to the rational, democratic person' – in the context of 'you too can learn to be a writer' – the approach can also, the authors rightly note, 'be abused by plot wheels, formulaic writing, and how-to-books that taken to the nth degree suggest that writing is pure craft' (p. 313).

In fact, a good deal of promotion for New Criticism's evaluative and taxonomic language of craft and technique still comes in the form of creative writing 'how-to-books', guided textbooks not so far removed from the syllabic texts of the 1930s. This particularly holds true for *Understanding Poetry*, its sections punctuated with close readings of the poem 'as poem'. The text went through its fourth edition in 1976 (which shows the long-lasting nature of New Criticism's effects), and its companion volume *Understanding Fiction* (1943) followed the same close analysis of language and structure. Cleanth Brooks published *Modern Poetry and the Tradition* – sometimes cited as the best introduction to the New Criticism – in 1939. Two years later, *New Criticism* appeared as the name of John Crowe Ransom's 1941 text (Graff, 1987: 153), and though the movement may have peaked in literary history, its insidious practice remains dominant in the creative writing classroom.

Pick up almost any creative writing handbook to find a table of contents neatly compartmentalized into 'Elements of Fiction' (plot, characterization, setting, point of view, voice) or 'Elements of Poetry' (meter, metaphor, rhythm, rhyme, style) as the case may be, complete with a synopsis of each craft element (best practices, pitfalls, what to consider, define, describe, differentiate, explore) – a virtual 'how-to', followed by exemplary stories or poems that model the elements of craft. As a graduate student, teaching her own undergraduate workshops, Pollack discovered that dozens of textbooks and anthologies were modeled along the lines of *Understanding Fiction*. A good example of a New Criticism prescriptive style is Janet Burroway's 2007 handbook, titled *Imaginative Writing: The Elements of Craft*, a popular textbook for classroom usage. Pollack also notes that no matter how much she encourages students to ignore/rebel/change up the covenants of New Critical techniques in her own creative writing classes, 'the principles that Brooks and Warren set forth in *Understanding Fiction* still exert a powerful influence on any writer who comes anywhere near the academy' (Pollack, 2007: 547).

I certainly do not dispute the importance of close reading or craft-based pedagogy as these rudiments work well for beginning students. Additionally, a case can be made that there is an element of relief for students who workshop their peers' stories in that the attention is on the text rather than the author who sits just a desk or two away in the same circle as they do. The most significant objection to the New Critical approach is that there seems to be a tendency for many teachers to rely on the study of craft in its simplest form, and in doing so there is an expectation that students will imply from the attention placed on the text that the techniques and conventions presented are always examples of the kind of 'good writing' expected in their own writing performances.

The ease of teaching the New Critic approach

Part of the dominance and popularity of New Criticism in the field of academic criticism in university English departments in the early to mid-20th (and later) century can be traced to its ease of teaching such that any need for prerequisite knowledge and/or course preparation is minimal. Haake (1994: 77) reports such an ease when she says, 'What could it take, after all, to sit around in a circle and explain to my students how to make their stories better'. Christopher Clausen (1997: 55), author of 'Reading closely again', considers that 'any student with an interest in literature, regardless of a presence or absence of a background in any other field of study, could become proficient in the New Critical method'. Correspondingly, Clausen reports, 'no professor of literary studies was required to subtract from the study of literature in order to impart these backgrounds to his students' (p. 55). Gerald Graff (1987) comments on what he has seen as the dependence of New Criticism as a necessary support for teachers. He cites his own teaching experience as an example, noting:

> [I]t was perhaps the instructors who needed the New Criticism most ... From my own experience ... in a stepped up PhD program of the early sixties, I can testify that usually I was lucky to be one evening ahead of my undergraduate classes. I remember the relief I experienced as a beginning assistant professor when I realized that by concentrating on the text itself I could get a good discussion going about almost any literary work without having to know anything about its author, its circumstances of composition, or the history of its reception. Furthermore, as long as the teaching situation was reduced to a decontextualized encounter with a work, it made no difference that I did not know how much the students knew or what I could assume about their high school or other college work – just as it made no difference that they had no more basis for inferring anything about me than I had about them. Given the vast unknowns on both sides of the lectern, 'the work itself' was indeed our salvation. (pp. 178–9)

Similar to Graff's discussion, William E. Cain (1984: 101) claims that from day one of a creative writing course, 'teacher and students can read and respond to poems, exchange views about tone, paradox, and imagery, and make discriminations about relative degrees of complex thought and feeling in texts'. Whereas Graff appreciates the ease of teaching from the New Critical perspective, W.E. Cain admires the 'democratic' functionality of this practice. He contends 'teacher and students gather round a common object, and all strive to give the most detailed and sensitive reading possible. Such a method quickly enables the student to feel accomplished as a "reader". He or she is empowered to see the writers' techniques or elements of craft'. Cain suggests this leads students to 'experienc[e] the pleasure of a new kind of expertise' (p. 101).

Evaluation

J.E. Spingarn, who first provided the name 'New Criticism' in 1910, posits that the central question of criticism (of any art form) asks, '[h]as [the artist] or has he not created a work of art?' (qtd. in Myers, 1996: 113). Allen Tate asks a similar question: 'What as literary critics are we to judge?' (qtd. in Cain, 1984: 14). For the New Critics, evaluative criterion for judging what is 'good writing' is not based on the subjectivity of taste. Rather, the determination of a 'work of art' is conducted according to a set of standards. Questions of whether an artist has created a work of art are answered by New Critics through an analysis that considers if 'the work has the same sort of stable and "objective" status as a language, [which] exist[s] in a "collective ideology", governed by enduring "norms"' (Lynn, 1990: 259). For example, a close reading reveals 'how the formal elements of the literary work, often thought of as a poem, create and resolve tension and irony' (Lynn, 1990: 259). The valuated 'norm', in this case, is that '[g]reat works control profound tensions' (Lynn, 1990: 259). As such, these types of standards, and only these standards, would be the ones upon which a poem would be measured as having value and worth.

To add to this, the ultimate goal to ascertain a text's meaning by offering a close analysis of the text is made possible by way of an exemplary reader. To take this one step further, not only is the text seen as the final authority of such determination, but its exemplary reader, through her elicitation of the text's meaning, is viewed as the final authority as well. When a teacher places meaning solely on the text in the composing process, she gives the text final authority in the evaluating practice, and she claims herself to be the final authority as an exemplary reader.

Evaluating the text as final authority

The problem with a New Critical approach is one of perspective. The text exists in isolation, as words on the paper, never as an incomplete work, but rather, according to Edward White, as a finished product 'in general in order to be criticized' (qtd. in Bizzaro, 1993: 236), particularly, Bizzaro (1993: 236) tells us, 'when held alongside what Nancy Sommers calls an "ideal text"'. Additionally, a New Critical approach becomes complicated because whenever a text is objectified or is perceived as final authority, the reading of student work and the workshop dialogue that follows traditionally silence the author. This silence is witnessed as a consequence of the overt discussion of students' poems and stories but also in the exclusion of any possible biographical coincidence the writer may have to the speaker of a poem or a fictional character in a story. In other words, no authorial intent or biographical nature, let alone social or cultural contextualization, embraces or implicates the author. This type of singularly focused reading of the student text does not 'grant to the student possible intentions or insights not yet present on the page' (Edward White qtd. in Bizzaro, 1993: 53).

While Mayers (2005) does not suggest that 'all creative writing teachers bring New Critical sensibilities to their classroom', he reports that his:

> experience in creative writing classes has been governed by the implicit understanding that the student text, though worthy of intense scrutiny

and criticism, should be conceived as occupying a sphere all its own, largely outside the bounds of economic, social, and material realities, largely outside of any rhetorical relationship to the world in which it presumably must operate. (p. 139)

With this method, there is ease in avoiding social and political implications when the focus is 'so sharply on the student text as to obscure any questions about whether, and how, the individual student text might fit into a larger textual network' (Mayers, 2005: 139). Indeed, New Critic advocates might accuse those teachers who permit social/historical commentary in the classroom of being authorities who possess the political clarity our students lack. In the effort to create political citizenry, some teachers enforce their own theories and determinations as justifiable and as evaluators of our students' work. Some teachers might ask what kind of vulnerable posturing do we insist (consciously or not) of our students but one that acquiesces to our view.

Prioritizing the text by giving the words on the page power proves limiting for groups of our students. For example, Nicole Cooley (2003: 101), who works at an urban multi-cultural public university, finds the New Critical reading strategy, which excludes extrinsic factors, to be 'problematic' for her class 'because many of her students have been silenced outside of the classroom for too long'. She sees the New Critical workshop practice as one that decenters her writers and prompts an unhealthy silencing of her students' differences.

The focus on the text as authority has caused poetry to become disengaged from a wider audience for those like Dana Gioia (1991) because this New Critic perspective perpetuates through academia. If what Gioia says is true in his essay 'Can poetry matter?' then teachers might consider taking time outside of their workshop-centered classrooms (a coveted place where many vehemently hold is the only place where time can be spent on student writing) to explore ways in which their students' texts address/ represent aesthetic and political sensibilities. Chris Green (2001) suggests that, indeed, creative writing practitioners ought to explore extrinsic influences. He proposes that 'before asking how students can better write "good" poems', we should 'look beyond the gaze of the sublime reader and ask how students can write useful poems' (p. 159). By 'useful', Green means the writing of poetry in 'a workshop where the class readership acts to represent the rhetorical circumstances of interpretive communities outside the university' (p. 154). When teachers center their focus on the authority of the text, they foster a view of exclusion, a sort of blindfolding, which does not permit them to see the other kinds of external forces that may come into play in a students' reading and writing of creative works.

Rather than apply New Critical methods in her creative writing course, Cooley, for one, circumvents such blinders to the outside world when she extends the boundaries of the canonized works as the primary reading choice for a creative writing course. In this manner, she advocates a textually-based class 'in which students read other texts as models for their own work' (p. 191). As a result, the dialogue of these non-canonical literary texts (with 'literary' defined as culturally and/or historically valued) becomes a more appropriate location for which to 'stage the issues and teach our ways of reading for workshop'. David Radavich (1999: 111) agrees with this approach, insisting that in addition to teaching the 'particulars of form and evocative expression', creative writing courses 'worth their enrollment' should teach 'reading, critical thinking, and awareness of historical context'.

In considering extrinsic properties that might influence the ways our students read and write texts, teachers might attempt to contextualize stories or poems at other levels once a discussion of the architecture is complete: its use of language and the choices writers make related to point of view, scene construction, voice, dialogue, characterization, setting and plot structure as they apply. A creative writing class might, for example, read Charlotte Perkins Gilman's (2000) 'The yellow wallpaper' from a sociological, political or psychological perspective, extending considerations beyond the tale of insanity. Students could talk about the struggle against the wallpaper's 'bars', the women lost in its 'torturing' pattern, the challenge of 19th century patriarchal ideologies and these influences in the design of such a story.

By extension, a creative writing class could segue from professional stories to their own by letting the fiction they read resonate with their own stories. To avoid reading the text as final authority, we might link stories with our own, talk about their social impact and the cultural and historical considerations that influence what and how we write.

We might surpass a linear reading of professional stories by taking our discussions beyond the summary of the plot, the description of characters and the elements of craft when we consider the creative work as a textual sphere, one which has a multiplicity of readings, contexts and relationships with the public world. We might choose some specific facet, some internal aspect, and compare it to other stories. The cosmetics of death, for example, its variance from culture to culture and from person to person are central in stories like Amy Hempel's (1983) 'In the cemetery where Al Jolson is buried', Leo Tolstoy's (1886) 'The death of Ivan Ilych' and Tim O'Brien's

(2007) 'The things they carried', and these stories can trigger – if they are presented as a collage of variable social, historical and cultural concepts – a broader range of relativity for our students than their study as textual objectification. Students also learn to develop rhetorical perspectives when they write brief essays in which one story is viewed in light of another, and in this manner the study expands into the public realm and 'reflection on the very enterprise of creative writing as it relates to larger social, political, and rhetorical trends' (Mayers, 2005: 48).[1]

When teachers and students challenge the exclusivity of the text as final authority then more variable approaches to reading and writing can open spaces for more experimentation and direction. Such an inquiring perspective leads us to question the view of the text as final authority, to ask '[w]hat can we learn from literary criticism and theory if we approach creative writing with a more inclusive pedagogy?' (Cooley, 2003: 103). We should also ask how we might challenge literary codes. Who decides what makes for good writing? Who decides 'what is a poem? What is a story? What is a play?' Instead of implanting 'in our students a set of unexamined values for them to deploy in their own work', Cooley's class, for instance, discusses what makes 'good writing' as they examine the confines of the canon. She encourages teachers to 'break the rules', 'reconfigure generic categories', 'challenge literary codes' (p. 103). Along the same lines, Haake (1994: 78) questions the text as verbal icon. She admits to previously wanting her students to 'view their texts as autonomous literary artifacts, separate from their real selves and subject to analysis'; and so she began, considering how Francois Camoin once began with her by noting 'if you want to build a funhouse, a set of working blueprints would prove useful' (qtd. in Haake, 1994: 78). But then Haake worried over 'her students struggle to analyze their own textuality' (1994: 78). In her response to Scott Russell Sanders' urging that we 'concentrate on "artistic criteria" as the only aspect of writing over which we have any "control"' (qtd. in Haake, 1994: 85), Haake justly interrogates, 'Whose criteria are these? Where did they come from?' (1994: 85).

Teacher as final authority, as exemplary reader

In Bizzaro's comprehensive view of the ways teachers respond to students' texts in *Responding to Student Poems* (1993), he notes his sense that teachers have historically appropriated their students' writings, and that part of this concern is secondary to the limited attention paid to the ways in which we provide feedback to students' work. In an effort to avoid the appropriation of students' texts, where 'values are the values expressed in most teachers' interpretations of their students' texts', Bizzaro applies theories 'heretofore employed only with "sanctioned" literature' as a reading strategy when he reads and evaluates students' poems (Bizzaro & McClanahan, 2007: 85). He references Alberta Turner's findings in *Poets Teaching* (1980), a collection of student work and teacher responses, to show us that most poet commentaries advance a text-based approach to interpreting students' poems. One contributor in this collection offers that:

[T]eachers tend to view the poem as an entity in isolation, 'a little world of words', which either engages the reader and is deemed a success or fails to engage the reader and, as a result needs to be revised. Second, teachers tend to assert the authority of the exemplary reader when they model a teacher-centered method for teaching revision skills. (Qtd. in Bizzaro, 1993: 42)

An example of this teacher assertion located in Turner's collection of responses is the instructor who 'takes the student poem as his own and verbalizes changes he would make to the text if the poem were his' (qtd. in Bizzaro, 1993: 42). Another illustration is Paul Cook's (Cook *et al.*, 1989: 247) technique of 'tak[ing] a blue pencil [in an effort to transfer his copyediting skills to the student] and escort[ing] the student through his or her story in an attempt to cultivate, in that *student*, the value of good editing'. Richard Hugo defines the exemplary reader perspective when he says, '[i]f I can, I talk as if I'd written the poem myself and try to find out why and where it went wrong' (qtd. in Bizzaro, 1993: 55). These illustrations demonstrate New Critical values, presenting the teacher as exemplary reader and ultimate authority. With New Critical values, 'the teacher's authority arises from reading a large number of other poems in a wide range of forms and styles' (Bizzaro, 1993: 42), and so this readerly experience can give way to an autogenetic appropriation of her students' work.

What happens when New Critical values are put into practice with student writing? Bizzaro notes that an 'unwanted though mostly unavoidable by-product of using the text-based methodology' (1993: 23) occurs when 'teachers do what seems most natural and instinctive in the traditional classroom: quickly provide students who have not had adequate reading experiences with the information they need to write poetry' or fiction in the form of text appropriation (1993: 23). He refers to composition theorists Sommers, Brannon and Knoblauch, who 'have argued that such appropriation is unwanted since it takes the authority for writing away from students, subordinating them to the authority of their masterteachers' (1994: 239). Sommers, he reminds us, 'found that teachers employ many of the same kinds of comments when responding to student writing from the New Critical perspective', noting there was, in fact, 'an accepted, albeit unwritten canon for commenting on student texts' (1993: 42). Bizzaro notes the functionality of these tasks:

> First they respond primarily to textual matters. Second, they tend to encourage a view of revision as text manipulation. Naturally, if misused (or used at the wrong place in the writing process), such comments can easily enable a teacher to appropriate a student's text, since only one text exists, the one the teacher reads and thus rewrites. (1993: 42–43)

In an effort to model for students the critical role he assumes when he asks questions of his own writing, Bizzaro demonstrates what happens when he uses the New Critical approach in reading and evaluating his students' poems. What he discovers, in the end, is that the New Criticism method of evaluation is limiting and less effective. The New Critical emphasis on the text requires him 'to use [his] energies to make intertextual comments' (1993: 53). What he finds is that his margin comments 'asked questions intended to reinforce intertextual comments, and [his] summaries in turn reinforced those questions' (1993: 53). The result of these kinds of comments, however, is that students can simply make the adjustments [he] urges[s] and resubmit the poem as finished' (1993: 54).

He adds, that '[t]his outcome might have been expected given the New Criticism's original goal: to interpret finished texts'; however, he 'tended to do much of the work for these students, perhaps in the hope that they would learn from making such changes and apply what they learned in the revision of other poems' (1993: 54). These corrections that are made by many of us are seen by students as roadmaps for 'good writing'. The logic is that where we spend our time (and in this case, it is with the text) is also where our students form their interpretations of what is 'correct writing'. Moreover, Bizzaro notes that with 'an ineffective adaptation of the New Criticism, a teacher might inadvertently require students to write in a narrow range of poetic styles' (1993: 54). The downside to this is that teachers dictate, as Anthony Petrosky says, 'stylistic limits that act to seal off ... students' writing, to keep it within the boundaries of academic expectations' (qtd. in Bizzaro, 1993: 54).

Social Relations: Through a Lacanian Lens

When a teacher's pedagogy privileges meaning in the isolation of the text, when she situates herself as exemplary reader and authority, and when she values and rewards student dialogue and written work based on her New Critical practice, she influences the social dynamics of the creative writing classroom and, in particular, the relationship between teacher and student. I propose that Jacques Lacan's (1966) psychoanalytic theories of the Imaginary and Symbolic orders can assist in explaining the complexities of the teacher-student role in the New Critic classroom. Briefly explained, before entrance into language and the Symbolic order, a child becomes fascinated by her own image in a mirror. The baby learns that this image is her own, recognizing that this image is a whole entity instead of fragmentary movements (the bits and pieces) and undefined boundaries between self and Other (the mother, specifically). The child situates herself in relation to the image and first knows herself as lacking. The infant forms an illusion of an ego, of a unified conscious self identified by the word 'I'. To Lacan, ego (or self) is always on some level a fantasy, an identification with an external image, and not an internal sense of a separate whole identity. This stage marks the fundamental narcissism by which the human subject creates fantasy images of both itself and its ideal object of desire. Once a child enters into language and accepts the rules and dictates of society, she is able to deal with others. The Symbolic order is bound up with the superego and works in tension with the Real and Imaginary orders.

The forces and drives that underlie students' writing, reading and interactions are directly influenced by the realms of the Imaginary and the Symbolic orders. It helps to understand Lacan's theory of (mis)recognition, the split between the self and the mirror-image, because we can apply his psychoanalytic model to what happens when there are conflicting types of intentions in the classroom. More specifically, the Imaginary and the Symbolic orders can be seen in the types of relationships that exist between teacher and student in the form of transference and counter-transference. For Lacan, transference is best understood:

> ... as a dynamic structure located partly within a person and partly between people. On the one side is a 'divided self', a person ... who does not understand some part of her own action ... On the other side is an authority figure, a person whom the 'divided self' *supposes to know* how to interpret the behavior. The person who feels divided looks to the authority figure for interpretation ... When the figure responds by asking questions or being silent (as analysts are largely supposed to), the divided person tries to respond/interpret the behavior as she thinks the authority figure would. (Brooke, 1987: 681)

The important relationship then 'is largely *within* the divided person, since it involves a relationship between her conscious self and her projection or current understanding of the knowledge and purpose of the knowing authority' (Brooke, 1987: 681). To this end, transferring an image of the self onto the analyst, the 'divided' person finds in the Symbolic Other (the *Subject Supposed to Know*), an external means to express her inner dialogue. In this manner, according to Robert Brooke (1987: 681) who authored 'Lacan, transference, and writing instruction', 'the analyst serves as a mirror for the person'.

In student-teacher transference, the 'baffling behavior involved is writing' (Brooke, 1987: 682) or responding to a written work. Brooke tells us that the student is 'universally assumed *not to understand* what he has written ... The writing teacher is fancied ... to *understand* writing, to *know* what writing should look like, how it's supposed to work, what the student's errors "mean" and how to fix them' (p. 682). The writing teacher, as comparable to a therapist in this sense, 'is institutionally a version of the Subject Supposed to Know' (Brooke, 1987: 682). It is the individual student who places 'value' on the 'importance of the Subject Supposed to Know' because '[s]omehow he or she must trust that this person really is what the role says she is' (Brooke, 1987: 683). A student 'can always choose not to enter transference by refusing to trust' the teacher, and the teacher can 'be deceived' by the student's 'demand' to know what he should do (Brooke, 1987: 683). After all, how many of our students ask us to just tell them what they should say, what they should do? The biggest threat then, according to Brooke and Lacan, is related to trust.

Presumably, most transference relationships allow students to trust the teacher, making learning possible because often a student has an unconscious need that she presumes a teacher can fulfill. And often, when a teacher has gained a student's trust, or in Freudian and Lacanian terminology, has elicited a positive transference, the student will look to the teacher as someone who knows the truth and knows what is in the student's best interests even more so than the student. In this manner, the teacher becomes the sole, inviolate authority.

In the New Critic classroom, there is an unhealthy order of transference as the teacher is truly the sole, inviolate authority as her 'power of privilege [is] so totally unchecked by a second or third party' (Bizzaro, 1993: 5). The fact that the teacher privileges meaning in the text bears import on her teaching strategies, from the ways in which she devises her plan for teaching to the evaluation of her students' writing. As a result, the teacher exerts complete control, not only, as Crowley notes, 'doing most of the writing in the course', but also 'setting rigorous laws for students to abide by' (qtd. in Bizzaro, 1993: 5). Crowley notes that while teachers do most of the writing:

... students, on the other hand, spend most of their time reading: they read the teacher to determine what he 'wants'; they read the textbooks or anthologies he has assigned to find out what he wants them to know; they read his assignments to determine what he wants them to do. When they 'write' in response to his assignments, they tell him what they think he wants to see realized in their papers. Almost never do they envision themselves as having something to teach their teachers. (Qtd. in Bizzaro, 1993: 6)

While Crowley applies these concerns to the composition class, the New Critical pedagogy can also have immediate concerns for students attempting to reconcile their Imaginary and Symbolic orders in the creative writing classroom. If we follow Lancanian principles, the student never enters into a contest of trust and the teacher does not question her role as the Subject Supposed to Know. The student cannot work through the writing and learning process because the New Critic teacher resists this permitting as she directs and appropriates what goes on in the classroom.

It becomes difficult for students to thrive in a master-teacher-student-apprentice model, one in which many workshop models are based. Haake (1994: 80) reminds us that '[s]ince the first classes were developed at Iowa, teaching creative writing in America has largely conformed to the model of a text-centered workshop where apprentice writers come together to craft poetry, prose, and drama and offer it to peers and the master writer'. In this workshop model, the authority of the text meets the teacher as exemplary reader. Case in point – W.D. Snodgrass (1999) speaks of his master-teacher Robert Lowell at the Iowa Workshop, as a 'powerful' mentor. When Lowell 'did' your poem, said one student:

... it was as if a muscle-bound octopus came and sat down on it. Then, deliberately, it would stretch out one tentacle and haul in mythology, a second for sociology, a third for classical literature, others for religion, history, psychology. Meantime, you sat there thinking, 'This man is as mad as they said: none of this has anything to do with my poor, little poem!' Then he began tying these disciplines, one by one, into your text; you saw that it did have to do, had almost everything to do, with your poem. (Qtd. in Snodgrass, 1999: 127)

Although somewhat theatrical in his dramatic sweep through his student's poem (though this element certainly adds to the mentor's power and mystique), Lowell is perceived by his student(s) as final authority, certainly as master-teacher. Alberta Turner affirms this relationship between teacher as master and student as apprentice when she says, '[t]o the student-poet as artificer the teacher-poets give (or rather offer) advice from their own experience as artificers' (qtd. in Bizzaro, 2004: 237). Bishop's scholarship has referenced this dominant teaching model as well, which we know continues in undergraduate and graduate courses today, and Ostrom recognizes the perception of writer-teacher as one who 'is important, authoritative, powerful' (1994: xiv).

Although Snodgrass' account of Robert Lowell may not have been all that atypical for master-teacher-student-apprentice workshop scenarios at Iowa, Carol Bly (2001) suggests that as master-teachers, teachers risk becoming bullies. Beginning writers, Bly says:

> ... give their souls into their work. They are very vulnerable. They believe what teachers tell them. They shouldn't but they do. They honor our (teachers') seniority. Our judgments are probably worth a tenth of what students give us credit for. If we have the least weakness of ego or the least career-climbing corruption or the least inability to reject flattery from people around us, we are at risk to bully. When we are tired we might even do a little bullying without noticing. (p. 143)

If not by bullying, then perhaps as master-teachers, we hold our apprentice-students with a powerful hook. Richard Hugo (1979), for example, writes in *The Triggering Town* about the injurious repercussions of Theodore Roethke's master-teaching on apprentice-poet David Wagoner in this way: 'Roethke, through his fierce love of kinds of verbal music could be overly influential. David Wagoner', Hugo stipulates, 'who was quite young when he studied under Roethke at Penn State, told me once of the long painful time he had breaking Roethke's hold on him' (p. 29). This master–apprentice power along with the *singular* focus on the text – on the teacher as exemplary reader and inviolate authority – emphasizes the mystique of the writing process and the master-apprentice role. It risks tunneling our students' vision and placing (and keeping) our students in a dependent, rather than a collaborative, role in our classrooms.

New Criticism Theory: Final Arguments

In the workshop model, Bizzaro and McClanahan (2007: 86) worries that the master-apprentice relationships can lead to 'the teacher having near dictatorial control over their students' texts', to teachers deciding, even, a student's failure if she did not make the comments suggested. More often the appropriation is more subtle (but still present) and can and does lead to a 'generation of clones – students who sound amazingly like their teachers' (Bizzaro & McClanahan, 2007: 86). While New Critical values are present in our appropriation of students' texts – in our craft-based pedagogy, and in our workshop dialogue – many creative writing teachers, as exemplary readers and final authority, often see their images as far from this prescriptive description. The writing workshop class is not exactly the 'banking system of education' in which Paulo Freire's description of teacher as depositor and student as depository fits the creative writing classroom. The hopeful poet or fiction writer 'cannot simply sit and wait for the transfer of knowledge from teacher to student – Moses handing down tablets where the truth is etched in stone' (Elliott, 1994: 113).

Lad Tobin (2004: 79) insists we must 'shock' New Critics in the way we 'misread every student text in order to help students say what we think they really mean', so that 'when we read we create and recreate, deconstruct and reconstruct'. Tobin suggests:

> ... this sort of generous and deliberate misreading – readings in which we go beyond the words' literal meaning to try and draw out possibilities in a text, to imagine what the text might be trying to become – is at the basis of Shaughnessy's analysis of error, Elbow's believing game, and Bartholomae and Petrosky's plan to integrate reading and writing. (pp. 79–80)

We ask our students to 'show' us, rather than 'tell' us when they write. We need to follow this practice as well in our teaching. Bizzaro (1994: 234) argues that teachers 'must spend less time telling our students what they should do when they write and more time showing them who they can be'. First, we must be aware of the way we respond to our students' poems and stories, and then '[i]f our reliance on New Criticism shows a discrepancy between what we know we should do and what we do in actuality, then', Bizzaro (1993: 40) suggests, 'we need to explore new and more fruitful models for evaluating student writing'.

The Expressivist Theory
Historical Antecedents

In his attempt to yoke the individual and the democratic spirit imbued in the new progressive pedagogy, Elmer Edgar E. Stoll (1932: 296–297) conveyed 'art [as] a state of the soul, communicated'. Irving Babbitt would say in 1932 that *katharsis* has moved from the reader, where it properly belongs, to the writer. As a guiding principle of the expressivist theory, *self-expression* has its roots in the progressive education movement of the early 20th century, one which began as a 'concrete representation of an idea about the best way to teach literature' (Myers, 1996: 12), and one which, as a form of self-expression, presents in today's creative writing pedagogy. Progressive education's influence, according to James Berlin (1987b: 58), 'encompasses the best and the worst of the American experience'. Because there was a dramatic increase in prosperity during the twenties, followed by 'the economic catastrophe' of the depression, writing instruction during these years responded in 'curious' ways (Berlin, 1987b: 58). Subjective-rhetoric, for instance, 'celebrated the individual', and transactional approaches 'emphasized the social nature of human experience; both rivaled the current-traditional rhetoric present in the college classroom' (Berlin, 1987b: 58). These studies and links of science to human behavior shaped the curriculum of progressive education.

As a result, psychology principles affected the shift from 'subject-centered to a child-centered school' (Berlin, 1987b: 59), while sociological maxims influenced perceptions of group behavior. John Dewey attempted to reconcile these two diametric approaches to education – 'psychological and individualistic' and 'social and communal' (Berlin, 1987b: 60). Hughes Mearns – guided by Dewey's goal toward a transactional rhetoric for a democracy and by his belief 'that the aim of all education [was] to combine self-development, social harmony, and economic integration' (Berlin, 1987b: 47) – shaped an expressivist curriculum, as head of the Lincoln School, the cradle of progressive education.

At this laboratory school, under the aegis of Teachers College at Columbia University, Mearns conducted a 'deliberate experiment' of replacing the subject of English for junior high school students with what he called 'creative writing'. Rather than continue with the 'over-emphasis on nature poetry' and its complex Romantic and Freudian poetics, which looked to nature for metaphoric associations, 'greater consideration would be given by teachers to themes more in harmony with the child's probable experience' (Berlin, 1987b: 78). For Mearns, the 'cry was that *subjects* should not be taught, *students* should' (Hughes Mearns, qtd. in Myers, 1996: 101).

As a literary movement, progressive education stimulated transactional approaches, emphasizing the social nature of human experience, and this led to essays on expressionistic rhetoric. Periodicals such as the 1922 volume of *English Journal*, soon touted 'all writing is art', 'writing can be learned but not taught', 'the content of knowledge is a product of a private and personal vision', and an emphasis of process over product in the composing transaction (Berlin, 1987a: 75–76). One such contributor, Allan H. Gilbert of Trinity College, argued that 'all honest writing – and no other sort is worth correcting – is the expression of the nature of the student' (qtd. in Berlin, 1987a: 76). Like the practices of Mearns and other progressive educators, Gilbert encouraged a non-directive method in the teacher as 'gadfly rather than dictator' (Berlin, 1987a: 76). For instance, teachers could not appropriate students' writing 'without bringing about a change to what was limited by their [students'] minds' (qtd. in Berlin, 1987a: 76). Primarily, students were to be encouraged to develop their own genius.

The charge of instruction was to remove cultural impediments to creative expression. One educator claimed, 'in a creative writing class almost any writing is better than no writing' (qtd. in Myers, 1996: 108). For Mearns (1935: 2), 'the best literary education comes with the amplest self-realization of the individual at whatever age he happens to be'. This setting free of the creative spirit took the form of poetry, a device students had difficulty with when the focus was on topics other than the self.

Because each student was so fundamentally isolated, his only recourse when writing was to delve into himself. 'Poetry, an outward expression of instinctive insight', according to Mearns, 'must be summoned from the vast deep of our mysterious selves. Therefore, it cannot be taught; indeed, it cannot even be summoned; it may only be permitted. As a result, the new education becomes simply, then, the wise guidance of enormously important native powers' (p. 28). Rather than teach students *how* a poem works or provide lessons on craft-based lexis or the critical study of literature and modeling approaches of professional writers, Mearns became concerned that an egalitarian relationship must exist between teacher and student. His pedagogical design employs a theory of education that includes a 'theory of permitting' and the teacher-artist as 'an ethical exemplar' (p. 28). This notion of the teacher as ethical exemplar is in contrast to the New Critical teacher as exemplary reader. While it was important to Mearns that teachers of creative writing were artists so that they might understand the creative process, the process of drawing out a student's creativity required a teacher-artist, an ethical exemplar, who had sensitivity and taste.

The underlying belief of Mearns that every student was at their core a poet becomes clear in his claim that 'each poet here has his own individual song' (p. 45). It was precisely this 'individual song', this internal unwritten work that permitted Mearns' egalitarian pedagogy and allowed him to sidestep the issue of talent in his teaching. What then distinguished one poet from another was not innate, undemocratic talent, but a patience to uncover the poem within. To Mearns and his students, then, the effort to bring these unwritten stories to the light of day was not a matter of craft so much as a matter of waiting and attentiveness.

In the 1930s William Faulkner would tell his interviewers that it is '[t]he material itself' that 'dictates how it should be written' (qtd. in Murray, 1989: 112), or as William Stafford has it, 'a book has always been something that grew and declared itself' (qtd. in Gudding, 1999). Even later, Moxley (1989: 40) would suggest that 'we need to treat all student writing as emerging texts', as a process of discovery.

The 'self' was also promulgated in 'how-to' books in the expansionist climate after World War II. Subsequent decades tended, among other precepts, to discuss the concept of 'self', in particular 'knowledge acquired outside the "self", a questionable attitude to reading, and continuous stress on self-expression' (Wandor, 2008: 104). The view of writing as an expression of the self became popular in the late sixties and early seventies with the focus on writing as a form of discovery advocated by such process pedagogues as Donald Murray and Peter Elbow.

As a second guiding principle of the expressivist theory, Romanticism has its roots in the 19th century as a movement away from the established social order. Even then, it promoted individualism and subjectivism, feeling over reason, intuition over intellect. Paul Dawson (2005: 27) goes back a bit further in his search for the evolution of 'creativity' and the general usage of the term 'creative' to a mid-18th century practice and 'the concept of man's creative power which motivated speculations about original genius, as opposed to imitative talent'. This led to a shift away from 'the classical learning of poets to their capacity for originality' then on to 'the idea of creativity as an expression of individuality and the twentieth century search for the "genius within"' (2005: 27).

There is a common link, Dawson decides, 'between nineteenth century poetry and twentieth century education, for the idea of poetic imagination which infused Romantic sensibilities also informed the Creative Writing movement which developed within the American school system in the 1920s' (2005: 50). It is here, at this juncture where the self-expressive theories of 'self', 'subjectivism', and 'discovery' interface with the Romantic sentiments of 'genius', 'imagination', and 'Divine power' under the broader theory of expressivism. The logic behind how these Romantic concepts found their way into the school system can be explained as a means to an end. Consider Mearns' philosophy in 'a belief in human creative power and its origins in the natural poetic abilities of the child' (qtd. in Dawson, 2005: 50–51) and link this to the poetic sensibilities addressed by Wordsworth and Coleridge in *Lyrical Ballads* to 'awaken a sense of wonder at the everyday by retaining and nurturing a childhood enthusiasm for natural surroundings' (qtd. in Dawson, 2005: 51). Dawson makes the connection for us when he says:

[I]f poetry was the means by which the special qualities of childhood were retained by the original genius, then poetry, or 'creative writing' was the means by which a child's creative potential could be developed before, in Wordsworth's phrase 'Shades of the prison-house begin to close/Upon the growing Boy'. (2005: 51)

The nurture of natural ability in students became the guiding principle for teachers.

In addition to the Romantic conception of poetic genius and Emerson's democratization of creative power, modern psychology and the latent unconscious creativity believed to be innate in all children, the development of self-expression and Romanticism as a creative writing outlet burgeoned in schools during the thirties. However, as an educational movement – its theory of permitting, writing to discover, self-expression, the rousing of poetic sensibilities – progressive education lost its centrality in the 1940s and 1950s when school reforms called for the learning of more basic skills. The movement rebounded in the 1960s and 1970s as a more radical version, touting free school movement and non-graded classrooms.

Present-day neo-progressivists hope to draw more interest in the fundamental principles of progressive education. While today's school systems are not guided by the principles of expressivism, creative writing, as a field and as a prospering university entity, continues to be invested in principles of self-expression and the sentiments of Romanticism. What continues is the belief that 'writing ability is fundamentally a matter of individual psychology or selfhood, something certain individuals are born with while others are not' (Mayers, 2005: 115). The central tendency for present-day teachers in the expressivist camp is to encourage personal discovery and to help students find their true selves and unique voices.

Pedagogical Practice

The pedagogical design of expressivism assigns the highest authority to the writer and her imaginative, psychological, social and spiritual development and how that development influences individual consciousness. Abrams summaries the expressivist process in this way: 'A work of art is essentially the internal made external, resulting from a creative process operating under the impulse of feeling and embodying the combined product of the poet's perceptions, thoughts and feelings' (Abrams, 1953: 22).

The material and the scope of the story or poem, therefore, are peculiarities/ singularities and the activities of the writer's mind. As such, expressivist pedagogy places the artist as the critical element in the composing process with the belief that it is she who not only creates the work but who establishes the criteria by which it is to be judged. Thus the teacher who privileges meaning *on* the writer (rather than on the text or reader or other imitable reality) is one who may neglect or discount any reductionist theories that contaminate the purity of writing. Expressionists believe that '[i]n its unintelligibility is [creativity's] splendor' (Boden, 2004: 14). In fact, Berlin (1987a: 484–487) tells us that '[t]hinking about how specific readers might react to a piece of writing, and trying to gear a piece of writing toward such readers, is folly for expressionists. They believe a truly great piece of writing will *find* its audience without conscious or specific intent by the writer'.

Moreover, the nature of expressivist teaching encourages originality (as manifested in the act of discovery) rather than imitation. Abrams's text *The Mirror and the Lamp*, from which my taxonomy of pedagogical theories parallels, notes the switch in the 19th century from the modeling of others to creating original work as a shifting from the mirror to the lamp. As a matter of fact, R.V. Cassill's *Writing Fiction* compares literature as an imitation of life to literature as 'an imitation or representation of the self' (qtd. in Wandor, 2008: 104) and cautions writers to stay true to their self-discovery. Cassill begins:

> ... as soon as we have learned something about our craft we are tempted to turn from concentration on our own experiences to the public world of great events – to write about spies and congressmen. But the first commandment is to go back stubbornly to our own field ... In the long run the reward for this may only be that the writer will discover who he truly is. (Qtd. in Wandor, 2008: 104)

Discovery and inspiration

The teacher who favors the inspirational approach of Romanticism 'sees creativity as essentially mysterious' (Boden, 2004: 14). Certainly, Plato, whose philosophical and interpretive challenges included his scholarship on rhetoric and poetry, expresses this view when he defines an artist. He claims, '[a] poet is holy, and never able to compose until he has become inspired, and is beside himself and the reason is no longer in him ... for not by art does he utter these, but by power divine' (qtd. in Boden, 2004: 14). Brent Royster (2005), who has written about the Romantic myth in the creative writing classroom, admits the following in his training as a writer:

I've come to relish time spent at the computer, especially when the work I do is impelled ('inspired') rather than compelled ('forced') ... If I'm working on a poem when such a sensation arises, my judgment about word choices, sounds, connotations and structures seems finely tuned and natural. During such periods, I've drafted page after page of work, and have been driven to a frenzied state while pounding keys, pacing, and reading work aloud. (2010: 105)

I do not think that I would be far off to suggest that most of us have experienced these fluid writing moments, and we do not likely question their source when they come. Inspiration for Wordsworth came in the form of 'an impulse from a vernal wood', and Whitman discovered he must 'lean and loaf and invite his soul' (qtd. in Blythe & Sweet, 2008: 311). Others required external stimulants to rouse the muse. For Poe it was drugs and alcohol. Coleridge insists ' "Kubla Kahn" was the product of an opium dream.'[2] Royster (2010: 105) describes his personal account of Romantic inspiration as 'palpable', 'almost addictive', and 'pleasurable'; he is not surprised that such 'dramatic, even romantic narratives of the writing process are prevalent'. Psychologist Mihaly Csikszentmihalyi recognizes such a flow state, 'in which a person's performance and mood have peaked', and he refers to these periods as 'autotelic experiences' (qtd. in Royster, 2010: 105). While Royster (2005: 32) clarifies inspiration as a 'dynamic set of forces coming together', he also confirms a writer's moments of seemingly inspired words on the page, which is an axiom teachers in the expressivist camp affirm and infuse into their pedagogies.

Expressivists may believe that they have a primary responsibility as teachers to awaken their students' sleeping muse and to help them discover not only their potential as writers, but who their students are under all the artificial layers of socially-assigned labeling. Such a cathartic process – through writing, through reading, through discussions – can feel rewarding for teachers and illuminating for students. Certainly, the strategy of having students look within themselves for creative material (the perception of writing as a form of self-cultivation) is a property which transcends to the expressivist classroom.

The inner processes at work in Royster's example are concepts that Madison Smart Bell contends is neglected as a teaching approach in creative writing. 'The great defect of craft-driven programs', he insists 'is that they ignore the writer's inner process. Creativity, the inner process of imagination, is not discussed' (qtd. in Blythe & Sweet, 2008: 311). Even the Iowa Writer's Workshop website, with its claim that '[t]hough we agree in part with the popular insistence that writing cannot be taught, we exist and proceed on the assumption that talent can be developed, and we see our possibilities and limitations as a school in that light',[3] privileges inspiration as a driving force of creativity, talent as innate and creative writing as an individual pursuit.

The expressivist workshop

One of Mearns' pedagogical terms for creative writing's league with progressive education is that 'the individual speaks out in his own voice' (qtd. in Dawson, 2005: 56). This tenet would become a prominent expressivist underpinning in the contemporary writing workshop, a space where Myers reports most workshop-based classes 'resort to "subjective expressionism"' (qtd. in Bontley, 2007: v). The physical arrangement of the workshop encourages this subject expressivism partly because, '[u]nlike professors in any other discipline ... We don't lecture or use the podium. We arrange our desks in a circle and tell our students they can call us by our first names ... many of us ... would prefer we eliminate grades altogether or establish a pass/fail policy for creative writing classes' (Cantrell, 2005: 65). Far from responding as teachers with inviolate authority, 'we are much more comfortable being the cheerleader, the midwife, the coach, or whatever than we are being the authority, the master-writer, the critic, or the judge' (Cantrell, 2005: 70). Royster (2005: 37) specifies that 'the creative writing workshop can facilitate the formation of self and voice' through 'multimodal, multivocal exploration of text and craft', *not* by 'Romantic illusions of the writer's life'.

What to do about the Romantic myth

Predominant Romantic and inspirational myths view the process of writing as enigmatic and seductive, 'intrinsically unpredictable', and paradoxically difficult to define, for 'how it happens is indeed puzzling', and yet, 'that it happens at all is deeply mysterious' (Boden, 2004: 11). The artist then is seen as gifted, imbued with creativity; writing comes easily – needing just a measure of prodding or inspiration to come forth. Such myths that surround the creative process suggest to students that the writing process does not require much work, practice or revision. Chad Davidson and Gregory Fraser (2006: 21), who attempt to dispel the Romantic and inspirational myths that surround – in this case – the writing of poetry, insist that '[b]elieving these myths about artistic creation means accepting the premise that some of us are merely "hardwired" for creativity and that it cannot be learned'.

Burroway offers a version of the inspiration model when she encourages freewriting because '[m]any writers feel themselves to be an instrument through which, rather than a creator of, and whether you think of this possibility as humble or holy, it is worth finding out what you say when you aren't monitoring yourself' (qtd. in Leahy, 2005: 65). When talent is considered natural, when inspiration is our source of creativity and meaning, and when recursive processes are interrupted or ignored because the initial piece was 'inspired' and therefore not reducible in any re-envisioning process, the expressivist classroom depreciates to a Romantic model of permitting. A model that 'doesn't risk the active self in the writing process' engages the students who think they can already write or those who are 'most concerned with self-esteem' (Leahy, 2005: 61). David Galef (2000: 170) claims the 'aura of the isolated artist' still 'shines among the general populace' in our cynical age of spin, marketing and audience. Even '[i]f much of this feeling is misguided', Galef offers, 'the enthusiasm of dilettantes... nonetheless drives enrollments up' (p. 170). Royster (2005: 27) also situates this Romantic portrayal of the writer 'wholly dissociated from society', as one, he suggests, who 'invests the craft of writing with particular gift and purpose' in the contemporary classroom. Moreover, he sees this same phenomenon within popular creative writing journals such as *The Writer's Chronicle* and *Poets and Writers*. He notes how these journals can mystify student writers because they imply creative writing cannot be taught, that talent is inherent, that student writers 'need to be individual, gifted, prolific', which leads to 'some writers [who] hope to be talented before being taught, before developing discipline, even before becoming writers' (2005: 27). These Romantic notions are proliferated by 'anecdotes of extra-worldly creative prowess', such as the rumor that Jack Kerouac wrote *On the Road* in a matter of weeks, 'furiously typed on paper ingeniously taped together to form one long scroll' (Royster, 2005: 27). Anna Leahy extends this Romantic view to students who enter our creative writing classrooms with what Anne Lamott calls 'the fantasy of the uninitiated' in which '[p]eople tend to look at successful writers ... and think they sit down at their desks every morning feeling like a million dollars, feeling great about who they are and how much talent they have and what a great story they have to tell' (qtd. in Leahy, 2005: 56)

Leahy (2005: 56) notes that 'Our students want to be those writers and seek a place where they can foster that desire'. Adding to this mindset is 'the Romantic model of inspiration', which Leahy explains is one in which 'the author is perceived to lack any real effort, or any real responsibility for her own poems or stories'. In other words, writing isn't considered 'real work' (2005: 61). Royster (2005: 37) advances this concept when he proposes 'the creative writing workshop can facilitate the formation of self and voice' through 'multimodal, multivocal exploration of text and craft', *not* by 'Romantic illusions of the writer's life'.

Romantic myths can also suggest that there are secrets to the writer's craft, secrets which if revealed 'would most surely corrupt [the artistic] process beyond recognition' (Vanderslice, 2006: 149). One of the questions I asked creative writing teachers in my workshop survey was how they kept the workshop alive and robust in their classrooms. One teacher resisted sharing her workshop practices, noting, 'I'm not about to reveal my secrets'. As a whole, though, keeping craft secrets seems less of a problem in contemporary creative writing classes. With the process-based model and writers writing about writing, the writing process is exposed in articles, collections, interviews and public addresses. More and more we're demystifying the creative writing process and sharing our pedagogy with others in a more visible and concrete way.

Can then, the sensibilities of the Romantic myth ever be a positive influence in our students' writing? I propose that it can for at least two reasons: first, the Romantic myth values creativity and creative writing. This is enough to motivate students, to give them courage to enter our 'creative' writing classrooms. It lets us acknowledge 'creativity' as an important and serious business. Creativity requires work, practice, reading – its antithesis is an opposition to labor or the idea that words spring forward on the page as Muse-blessed. Chad Davidson and Gregory Fraser suggest students might find it helpful to think of poetry (and fiction) writing in terms of sports or dance analogies:

> All the endless free kicks pay off during the game. All the formal dance moves, once internalized, come freely to the dancer performing on stage. One learns in order to unlearn. One internalizes in order to call forth one's knowledge without having to think about it. One naturalizes, embodies, enacts. (Davidson & Fraser, 2006: 21)

The authors suggest that part of dispelling Romantic myths is 'helping untrained writers to unlearn their preconceptions and biases regarding this very different use of language' (p. 21).

Additionally, to value creativity – as a positive Romantic myth – allows our students to take risks in their writing, to appreciate that the peers in their writing community are taking risks as well. Furthermore, the Romantic myth connects writing to beauty, truth and originality. To reflect upon the beauty of a literary work – its language, sounds, images and arrangement – is a refreshing consideration from the focus on the deconstruction or theoretical interpretation of literature. As such, our charge can become, in part, to validate the positive elements of the Romantic myth, whose theory strongly underpins creative writing. Such discussions on the origination of ideas are important in creative writing to weaken other myths such as 'talent is inherent and essential, that creative writing is largely or even solely an individual pursuit, and that inspiration, not education drives creativity' (Swander *et al.*, 2007: 15).

Social Relations: Through a Lacanian Lens

Some teachers embrace their authority as a means of working with students toward a therapeutic end. For example, Brooke employs the responsive teaching of expressivists Peter Elbow and Donald Murray by exploring a version of composition pedagogy as seen through the lens of Lacan's theory. It becomes clear to Brooke 'that these kinds of teaching strategies work because they connect some basic psychodynamic processes: the interplay between self and Other, especially when the Other is understood by the writer as the Subject Who Is Supposed to Know' (Brooke, 1987: 680).

Brooke's teaching strategy involves a 'non-directive' approach that 'forces writers to "figure it out themselves", to respond to their own text' (p. 680). This open-ended approach can give writing ownership back to students rather than recreate a text of the teachers' own making. Brooke likens his process of 'projection and response' to Lacan's theory of psychoanalytic transference. He facilitates the transference by remaining fairly silent, as an analyst might, patiently waiting for the student to anticipate what the teacher would say if she were answering Brooke's open-ended questions. For Brooke then the writer responds out of her developing sense of what authorities 'who know' about texts are likely to say: she responds to her projected ideas of what she thinks the teacher wants. Brooke's teaching strategy also opens space for Real order writing as he introduces confessional and other personal narrative essays in his classroom.

Along the same vein, first-year composition teacher Carol Deletiner (1992: 209) claims in her article 'Crossing lines' that 'her students are her comrades'. In her class, they 'spend a lot of time reading, writing, and talking about pain' (p. 209) – a practice which is a Lacanian Real order expression. Furthermore, Judith Harris (2001: 181), referring to the same notion of Real order, believes '[p]sychoanalytic pedagogy supports the idea that writing can be therapeutic and, therefore, more meaningful for the student in the long term than other socio-epistemic pedagogies developed for undergraduate writing courses'.

Likewise, Mark Bracher (1999: 175) points to the opportunities for Real order expression in the writing class through 'self-reflective student diaries, experiments with confessional writing', as well as '[w]riting about literature and other cultural phenomena'. He believes these venues can 'provide a space for these Real-register forces, if one has one's students explore their own visceral responses. Feelings expressed in a safe and productive way' (p. 175).

The difficult task for most practitioners, one that 'many teachers feel threatened by, is providing space for the real – that is, for students to experience, express, and examine their feelings and passions; their desires, revulsions, and enjoyments' (Bracher, 1999: 175). Opponents of a psychological pedagogy that draws on Romantic theory, recognize this same difficulty and are concerned with the lack of training in handling crises that may be perpetuated by our students' release of unconscious drives (or 'inspirations' to continue the Romantic language) and about the constraints of a class that meets weekly over the course of one semester. Nancy Welch (1996: 46) states 'writing teachers have good reason for resisting a construction of the classroom as counseling session and accepting the psychoanalytic concepts of "transference" and "counter-transference" as an unquestioned pedagogical good'. This position gives us pause to consider the statistics that suggest a significant percentage of our student population suffer from depression (and we cannot ignore the media attention to school violence and its 'supposed' connectivity to creative writing expression), and so it becomes difficult for many to assume a sentinel role (if in fact we do) for our university campuses as gatekeepers of our students' writing lives.

Welch also refers to Tobin's (1996: 33) notion that 'the dynamics of transference and counter-transference between student and teacher are most destructive and inhibiting in the writing class when we fail to acknowledge and deal with them'. She insists:

> ... it's also because of the destructive powers of transference – the potential misreading, misunderstandings, resentments, potential for abuse, and even psychic violence that can come with identifying one's self in another – that I can't join Tobin in saying, 'In my writing courses, I want to meddle with my students' emotional life and I want their writing to meddle with mine'. (p. 33)

Similarly, while Ann Murphy (1989: 178–179) admits that teaching writing elicits some of the same powerful forces of transference and resistance that psychoanalysis does, she urges that:

[I]t may be both foolhardy and dangerous to insist ... that a student probe his feelings about his father, his masculinity, and his grandmother's death, in the interest of provoking a more 'authentic' voice. We have the psychological and institutional power to elicit this matter, but neither the training nor the context to handle it.

She reminds others that 'we are serving as teacher/analysts, eliciting these unconscious forces and provoking this encounter with the enormities of language, in an institutional setting which aligns us as well with the less amiable third role in Freud's triad: government official' (p. 175).

While some admit that the familiar 'discourse of creative writing has been so thoroughly shot through with Romanticism' (Mayers, 2005: 116), that some teachers readily acknowledge its influence in their pedagogy, the difficult task for others is the threat of negotiating a place for Lacan's Symbolic Real – 'that is, for students to experience, express, and examine their feelings and passions; their desires, revulsions, and enjoyments' (Bracher, 1999: 175). Although we all know that students draw from their personal experiences (we all do) for their fictional accounts, the difficulty for many teachers is when students reveal, without any prompting, that their 'fictional' story is 'true'. Sometimes, the personal experiences they choose to signify make teachers uncomfortable because they can't know for sure if their students are prepared to deal with the sentiments that surface. How might a teacher delve into texts without misreading the gaps? The challenge of expressivist pedagogy is in the responding to bits and fragments of a student's life or, for another matter, the expectation by some that the teachers are to manage, in some small measure, the emotions gnawing away at the psyche of their students. While this type of writing may indeed be therapeutic, as Judith Harris concludes, some ask how teachers should respond once their students' egos are decentered or what they might do with residual and conflicted feelings that surface in their classroom.

Louise Rosenblatt acknowledges that when students read and write personally, they often reveal some of their 'conflict and obsessions', thereby tempting teachers to deal directly with these psychological issues. Although she points out some instances in which students have benefitted from this sort of interaction, she ends up warning teachers against 'officious meddling with the emotional life of their students' because 'teachers cannot be trusted in this sort of relationship' (qtd. in Tobin, 1991: 342).

Teachers are not exempt from the influences of their own personal issues and values – whatever they may be – and they carry these personal matters to their creative writing classrooms. Rosenblatt agrees that 'teachers are themselves laboring under emotional tensions and frustrations' (qtd. in Tobin, 1991: 342), while Murphy reminds us that teachers 'themselves are often untenured, part-time faculty – many of them women – whose relationship to their institution is fragile at best' (Murphy, 1989: 181). If it is unfair, unsafe even, for teachers to assume additional responsibilities, to act as 'Lacanian analysts, and potentially to endanger their jobs by deconstructing their classrooms', then, is it 'naïve or insensitive' to expect teachers to assume this role? (Murphy, 1989: 181). Yet, Tobin and others believe that 'the teaching of writing is about solving problems, personal and public' (1991: 342). Tobin does not think 'we can have it both ways: we cannot create interest and deny tension, celebrate the personal and deny the significance of the personalities involved (p. 342). It is an interesting dilemma, one which teachers face more often these days.

To the end that we can strengthen our students' identities; we can help them learn how to use the power of language to discover, create and communicate meaning. While we may not intend to 'meddle' in our students' lives, it is likely that we have done so to some degree. It is hard not to be affected when a student asks if she can leave 15 minutes early to pick up her birth control pills before the clinic closes or says during office hours that she missed the last three classes because she had an abortion, or when another student writes about his guilt because he should have known his best friend would commit suicide, or when another shares the first time she realised her sexual orientation was not heterosexual.

Recently, I judged an undergraduate writing competition. One well-written and painfully poignant memoir was about incest. The details were very specific and the legalities of publishing such a powerful piece were considerable as the case remained in litigation. The essay was eliminated from the contest because of this litigation issue, but the bottom line here is that our students' stories resonate with us whether we try to remain objective or whether we meddle or not. After all, we develop a sense of community in writing classes that only enroll 20 or so students; we place them in small group settings. We make it easy for students to open up.

Whether teachers support self-expression in their classroom or avoid it as best as they can, the issue of transference and counter-transference cannot be disregarded. How a teacher responds to a student about her writing or her behavior in class is infused with a teacher's own unconscious drives, desires and identifications, no matter how hard the teacher insists she remains objective. Adding to this point, Nancy Kuhl wonders what we, as teachers of authority, are to do 'with a model that ties art to personal well-being' (Kuhl, 2005: 11). Perhaps as an antilogy to New Criticism's reading and evaluation norms, there is the relativist notion that when the writing is self-expression, 'any creative work can be judged only with criteria specific to its making' (Kuhl, 2005: 11). This model (not so uncommon in creative writing classrooms today and quite distanced from New Critical values), renders – by virtue of its relativism – 'any classroom authority meaningless and may even eliminate the need for an instructor by eliminating all fixed criteria for judgment' (Kuhl, 2005: 11).

I agree with Tobin when he claims that we cannot deny the significance of transference in teacher-student relationships. After all, it is impossible not to be affected by our students and impossible for them not to be affected by us. We cannot 'focus on the writing process and product as if it existed in a decontextualized situation and relationship' (Tobin, 1991: 341). Yes, we may be uncomfortable acknowledging that we assume the role of the Subject Supposed to Know within our students' lives because the kind of 'unlocking' that occurs in students' writing and our response to such writing involves us in both transference and counter-transference. However, since transference and counter-transference involve images of the self and of others and student-teacher relationships, we need to decode more constructively what goes on beneath the surface of our writing instruction. Understanding Lacan's theories of the Real, Imaginary and Symbolic orders and the dynamics of transference and counter-transference is a good place to begin.

Expressive Pedagogy: Final Arguments

Romantic terms such as 'creative' and 'individual' and Platonic aims of 'beauty' and 'truth' are seldom questioned in the course of writing creatively. Certainly, it is often ingrained in our students' consciousness. Like Royster's students, writers in my introductory creative writing class are skeptical when the origin of work is called into question. They speak of inspiration originating from the heart or soul, especially with poetry writing. They want to write in abstractions, reflect in the 'self' and express vague emotions – sometimes writing long expositions on how a character or speaker in a poem feels. The problem with inspiration as a Romantic notion is one of ownership. If the writer is merely a medium through which the muse speaks, then who lays claim to the artistic work? Even professional authors are reluctant to deny that indefinite spiritual drive that allows each person to act.

In an effort to investigate alternatives to students' romantic consciousness, we should examine with our students where ideas come from, what triggers an image, an emotion, a character's actions. We should try to ground our students' romantic abstractions in reality, in concrete vivid details, in down-to-earth experiences and research. Bishop (1990: 64) practiced this when she asked students to list sources for their creativity – 'where they find their inspiration'. She told her students that she got writing ideas when she went running, shopping or from reading other writers. Such an assignment forefronts the ways that thoughts enter our minds, the logic and interconnectivity between germs of story/poem ideas, the formation through metaphors and images and language in general.

Students who enter creative writing classrooms often do so with popular images associated between writing and self-discovery. Kuhl employs useful and variable teaching strategies to minimize this perception. Of particular interest, she 'assign[s] readings by writers who discuss issues in question', and along the same lines, she 'invite[s] local and faculty writers to class to discuss their writing processes and their reason for writing' (p. 9). Readings and discussions such as these not only lend support to her claims that literary writing is a separate activity from writing, but they also shed light on the writing process as a complicated, recursive practice.

Two final points: first, in considering the degree to which Romantic theory persists, Dawson (2005) recollects the survey of 18th century theories that began my discussion. The emphasis, he reminds us, was on the artist as original genius and the creative power of the imagination. These theories led to how the phrase 'creative writing' (conceived by Emerson, named by Mearns), became 'associated with a lack of necessity of learning of any kind, with an ease of composition reliant on natural ability rather than the study of precepts, and with a sense of self-expression' (2005: 29). The association between Romanticism and its innate rather than learned behavior is partly responsible for the lack of understanding and misunderstanding of the ways in which the discipline functions in a critical academy. Dawson contends that 'when a course of study labels itself creative writing there are going to be complaints that writing cannot be taught, and that a university, a place of higher learning and of work, would seem antipathetical to the very concept of creative power' (2005: 29). Expressivist pedagogy advances this classification. Secondly, students in the expressivist classroom miss opportunities to learn others narratives and approaches when the practice of self-expression and Romanticism are the two dominant and current modes.

The Mimetic Theory as Imitable Functions
Historical Antecedents

Mimesis began as an explanation of art with the Greek sophists of the fifth century, but even before then, Socrates informs us that this primitive aesthetic theory is evident in '[t]he arts of painting, poetry, music, dancing, and sculpture' (qtd. in Abrams, 1953: 8). Modes of imitation are expressed in Aristotle's *Poetics* in 'Epic poetry and Tragedy, as also Comedy, Dithyrambic poetry' (qtd. in Abrams, 1953: 9). The belief that art imitates the universe continued long after Aristotle's *Poetics* through the 18th century when its properties were more narrowly defined by English critics. It was most popular in 16th century Italy as critics in their definitions of 'art' often included the representation of another work in comparison – as imitation. However, in the 18th century, English critics refined the definition of art in relation to a more select and narrowed range of imitable sources. Although imitation pedagogy was interrupted by Romantic concepts of language and the self as original, it still functions today in the pervasive modeling practices of our creative writing pedagogy.

Pedagogical Practice

The pedagogical design of mimetic or imitable theory privileges the concept that '[a]rt imitates the world of appearance' (Abrams, 1953: 8). Abrams suggests that this image of art as imitation, while it reveled in 'neo-classic aesthetics', did not play a dominant role in most theories. As such, it was more 'instrumental toward producing effects upon an audience' (p. 11).

One of the reasons why cognitive process theorists and social constructionists challenged the expressivist view in the eighties was that cognitivists and social constuctionists 'saw writing as a cognitive activity – that is, as a process of intellection students could learn how to do by imitating the behaviors of good or experienced writers' (Bizzaro & McClanahan, 2007: 81). In fact, Michael Pemberton (1993: 42) in 'Modeling Theory and Composing Process Models' suggests that 'the use of representational models as tools in scientific inquiry have become so widely practiced it can be considered a commonplace of empirical methodology'. In other words, modeling as a tool in scientific inquiry relates to creative writing as writers explore/imitate writing performances in various genres and publications, and this imitable praxis allows our creative writing students some basis of risk-free practice as well incremental steps towards knowledge acquisition, experimentation, and empowerment as students approach discovery and take authority for their own writing. Models help our students to conceptualize the world and the influx of stimuli that surrounds their lives.

Imitation help our students to identify and comprehend techniques and patterns of writing by experienced writers and that of established genre conventions as starting points from which to launch experimental practices and more autonomous practices.

Imitation or modeling as a workshop practice is the subject of Nicholas Delbanco's (2004) book *The Sincerest Form: Writing Fiction by Imitation*. While Delbanco does not attach the technique to the cognitive processes of the eighties (in fact, he goes back as far as the cradle for evidence of our mimicry), he does note that 'personal expressiveness', in this case, '[m]ay even be a mistake' (p. xxii), and '[i]n our pursuit of self-expression, we've forgotten the old adage that "[t]here's nothing new under the sun"' (p. xxiii). While cognitivists compared the revision practices of beginning writers to those of more experienced ones, most would agree that our task as workshop teachers often includes pointing out ways in which other more *experienced* writers have used particular techniques and storylines effectively. Delbanco refers to these techniques and practices as guides or routes 'to authenticity' (p. xxviii).

Imitation is an invention strategy that many creative writing teachers find effective in their classrooms today. It is effectual in the sense that students practice a particular style or learn techniques by mimicry. The downside to such use is twofold: published writing on this basis can add to the homogeneity of literature (Raymond Carver minimalism, Hemingway code of simplicity, Sylvia Plath confessional lyricism), and trying to aspire to 'greatness' may lead students to feel inadequate.

The writing prompts and models such as those found in Anne Bernays and Pamela Painter's (1995) *What If?: Writing Exercises for Fiction Writers* or *The Practice of Poetry: Writing Exercises From Poets who Teach*, edited by Robin Behn (1992), are imitative approaches in our pedagogy. While mimetic practices are very useful for students' practice of various styles and for helping the beginning students – who ordinarily might have trouble getting started – as a singular focus, this approach is limiting. One way to supplement and extend the practicality of their method is through student and group research and presentations. For example, demonstrations on the different kinds of submissions included in literary journals emphasize critical functions, explore market preferences and include creativity when exercises that imitate these variable styles for experimental purposes are employed.

Of particular interest to me is the impromptu assignment in which students write a poem (or story) appropriate for the literary journal. Mayers (2010: 103) has used such an assignment, and he notes that such mimicry of style might lead to a workshop of these poems, 'not in terms of any general or abstract aesthetic qualities, but rather in light of the specific things the class knows about the journal in question, based on the group project'. This is not an exercise in publication practices, but one Mayers finds 'to be particularly helpful in getting students to think (even if only at a crude and basic level) about how editors, as a potential audience, might be likely to view their work' (p. 103). While this has important reader-response implications, in its fundamental practice, it is based on imitative theory.

The premise behind mimetic pedagogy then is that students can comprehend writing strategies if they are to copy them. To appreciate how teachers privilege imitation in the creative writing classroom and how this practice impacts teaching, reading and writing, we might consider Jacques Derrida's practice of reading and rereading. He claims, 'It is necessary to read and reread those in whose wake I write, the "books" in whose margins and between whose lines I mark out and read a text simultaneously almost identical and entirely other ...' (qtd. in Minock, 1995: opening quotes). The teacher using mimetic theory underscores the principle that '[i]f you understand the way another's story has been built you can set about building your own' (Delbanco, 2004: xv). Building one's own stories or poems often begins with imitable practices in the creative writing classroom.

Social Relations: Through a Lacanian Lens

Lacan's insights lead to a better understanding of the importance and function of imitation in our pedagogy and in the social relations of our creative writing classrooms. In particular, in any dialogue on the subject of imitation it is important to keep in mind that 'language is not simply poured into listeners and readers as empty vessels, but translated in a process of rhetorical negotiation with an existing internal language, becoming – in Bakhtinian terms – "internally persuasive"' (Minock, 1995). This transition begins with the practice of language and style in imitable fashion. To what effect imitation is tied to Lacan's theorization of the mirror stage can once again be explained in relation to a child's initial entrance into language and the Symbolic order and the concept of transference. In brief, Lacan sees the self continuously developed in dialogue with others; conceptually, we nuance the language of others while trying to sort our identities. These unconscious exchanges manifest in the mirror relationship as the divided self looks to the teacher in this case (the temporary embodiment of the unconscious/the mirrored self) for answers or for information.

As such, the implications of Lacan's theory to pedagogy and to imitation are tied to the paradoxes that play out in these exchanges. As teachers, we help students to understand, assimilate and imitate when we delay the expectation that we are the ones who know. We also, if we accept the process of transference, resist the traditional academic response of filling up the empty vessels with consumable knowledge. The supplanting of our own authority 'and textual authority encourages students to engage in dialogues with texts, dialogues that are often based on unconscious desires' (Minock, 1995). In her essay, 'Toward a postmodern pedagogy of imitation', Mary Minock (1995) refers to these unconscious dialogues as 'properly irrational responses', and it is these responses that 'inspire in students a great attention to texts, a willingness to read and respond to them over and over again' [in Derrida fashion] and 'an *unpredictably* high incidence of imitation'.

Mimetic Theory: Final Arguments

Mimetic theory has its place in the creative writing classroom. We teach students to draw from the world and to practice the forms and techniques of others so that they can first recognize what is possible before they imitate it as practice and then make it original in its alteration or new construction. We open doors for students, let them look in the mirrors. In *The Art of Attention*, Donald Revell (2007: 8) speaks of the intimacy that comes from attention. He explains, '[i]t is the intimacy of poetry that makes our art such a beautiful recourse ... A poem that begins to see and then continues seeing is not deceived, nor is it deceptive'. Rather, he says, 'it is an intimacy in which creative writing and creative reading (the poet reads the world with writing) share together continuous presentations of this work ... ones and ones' (p. 8).

While the advantage of mimetic theory is of seeing and continuing to see, in reading the world, the student must eventually find her own sight. As Walt Whitman shares: 'you shall not look through my eyes either, nor take things from me/You shall listen to all sides and filter them from your self' (qtd. in Revell, 2007: 9).

The Pragmatic Theory as Reader-Response
Historical Antecedents

Reader-response theory has its roots in the late 18th and early 19th centuries before English literature became part of the academy's curriculum. Members of literary societies formed on college campuses and measured one another's responses relative to a piece they had all previously read. Jane P. Tompkins (1980: 206) links contemporary reader-response theory to classical commentaries on literature when scholars such as 'Plato, Aristotle, Horace, and Longinus all discuss[ed] literature primarily in terms of its effects upon an audience'. On a more formal basis, Eagleton (1983: 74) addresses 'reception aesthetics' or 'reception theory' as 'a fairly novel development'. He includes reader-response theory as one of three stages that marks the period of modern literature, citing the first as that of Romanticism and the 19th century in which there was 'a preoccupation with the author' (p. 74). This was followed by 'an exclusive concern with the text (New Criticism); and a marked shift of attention to the reader' (p. 74).

With this description, Eagleton contextualizes the history of modern literature in relationship to where meaning lies in the communication transaction. His classification is similar to Berlin's rhetorical triangle representation, Abrams's artistic transaction and my taxonomy of pedagogical theories. Reader-response theory is not clearly defined as a 'theory' of literary criticism, but rather as a theory of epistemology because it explains a way that a reader makes knowledge about a text.

Pedagogical Practice

Pragmatic theory as reader-response is aimed at the audience, for as Eagleton (1983: 74) says, 'for literature to happen, the reader is quite as vital as the author' (p. 74). This pragmatic theory considers, for Abrams (1953: 15), 'the work of art chiefly as a means to an end, an instrument for getting something done'. Stanley Fish (2005: 32) agrees when he says that meaning 'is an experience; it occurs; it does something; it makes us do something'. In *How Does a Poem Mean?*, written by John Ciardi (1959), meaning for a reader may begin with intrinsic sensibilities, that resonance that moves us in some way that is very human. Ciardi suggests that in poetry 'there is the step beyond: once one has learned to experience the poem as a poem, there inevitably arrives a sense that one is also experiencing himself as a human being' (p. 667).

Fish posits that meaning inheres not in the text but in the reader, or rather the reading community, when he says, '[i]n the procedures I would urge the reader's activities are at the center of attention, where they are regarded not as leading to meaning but to *having* meaning' (2005: 158). For Fish, there is no stable meaning in a text as its interpretation is variable from reader to reader and reading to reading. In its simplest form, the centrality of the reader-response pedagogy then is to teach students how 'to conceive a poem [or story] as something made in order to affect requisite responses in its readers' (Abrams, 1953: 15). I would replace Abrams's use of the word 'requisite' (as in 'required') to 'deserved' (as in 'entitlement') – to accentuate a more positive attitude that the text welcomes a reader's perspective. In fact, Eagleton perceives the text as 'no more than a series of "cues" to the reader, invitations to construct a piece of language into meaning' (p. 76).

Likely, because it is the newest approach, it is also not the one most privileged in pedagogy. It does, however, remove the writer from the lonely garret, recognizing instead that she is 'an agent within a social setting, and within an historical moment' (Royster, 2010: 105). This paradigm shift opens a space so that meaning might be placed on the reader in the composing process. Similarly, Vanderslice (2006: 147) acknowledges the solitariness of writing, and yet, she justly asserts, it is 'essential to learning that craft is the transformative understanding that one writes not only for self-expression but also to communicate to a reader'.

Moreover, Stephen Earnshaw (2007: 76) contends, 'it is not easy to navigate through the demands of self', and as such, writers prefer an audience for their material, a reader who has a 'sophistication of his or her art, a sophistication that is obviously felt to be lacking when the art is understood biographically'. Finally, when meaning no longer lies solely on the black marks on a page, according to some preconceived concept of 'good writing', then the text becomes 'inexhaustible, infinitely richer than any of its individual realizations because it is capable of different realizations' (Iser, 1978: 280). It is the interplay of reading (which is a temporal process) of 'sequential sentences which act upon each other without referring to an external reality', that offers meaning (Iser, 1978: 280).

The complexities of reader-response theory

Reader-response theory is a complex dynamic in the creative writing classroom for the process of reading is always in motion, always transposing. With this in mind, it can be claimed that Nancy Sommers' (1980) argument against the linear model of *learning* in 'Revision strategies of student writers and experienced adult writers' also applies to *reading*. In other words, we know that writing is not a straightforward linear process. It is, in fact, a revisionist cycle, what Eagleton calls 'the hermeneutical circle', a process of 'moving from part to whole and back to part', and reading loops in this way (p. 77). The reader brings to the work her own biases, beliefs, preconceptions, expectations and assumptions about universal truths (such as genre conventions). These influences interact with the reading of the work. In a sense, it might be said that students are reading themselves in the work – reacting, adjusting, picking up clues, processing and modifying their perspectives. As a student reads, she inserts herself into the reading, making inferences, searching for what Roman Ingarden calls 'a set of "schematic" or general directions, which the reader must actualize' (qtd. in Eagleton, 1983: 77). As a result of this process, the reader 'fills in the gaps' and 'tests out hunches', thus 'drawing on a tacit knowledge of the world in general and of literary conventions' (Eagleton, 1983: 76). What our students read in class, whether it be professional stories or their peers' incomplete stories or poems, are full of what Eagleton refers to as '"indeterminacies", elements which depend for their effect upon the reader's interpretation, and which can be interpreted in a number of different, perhaps mutually conflicting ways' (pp. 76–77). To require this kind of reading from our introductory creative writing students is not realistic. For one, the writing workshop model inadequately calls for students to know how to read as a writer and to prepare useful feedback to their peers' drafts. For another, teachers and students would need to make significant shifts from New Critical and Expressivist reading approaches to a more cooperative reading approach that considers both reader and text.

How to bring reader-response theory into the creative writing classroom

Although as readers we present with inferences, beliefs and expectations unique to ourselves, Wolfgang Iser's (1980: 79) reception theory – based on liberal humanist ideology – urges that we 'be prepared to put our beliefs into question, and allow them to be transformed'. In order to practice what Iser (1980: 79) calls a 'flexible and open-minded reading process' we might consider how a reader-response pedagogy prepares our students for this transformation. Iser speaks of the 'strategies', which texts put to work, and of the 'repertoires' of familiar themes and allusions which they contain. He contends that '[t]o read at all, we need to be familiar with the literary techniques and conventions which a particular work deploys; we must have some grasp of its "codes", by which is meant the rules which systematically govern the way it produces its meanings' (qtd. in Polkinghorne, 1988: 97). For the creative writing class, which is not governed by interpretive criticism, Iser's logic still has relevancy. Writers approach the reading of texts from a writerly perspective, and in doing so recognize the techniques employed by a writer and a text's codification in terms of *how* a story or poem is shaped to include the choices a writer makes and the effects that variable organizational principles and craft decisions have on the readability of the work. Learning how to read as a writer, to recognize the choices a writer makes, to appreciate the effects of these craft elements on the readability of the story and to imagine what might be different, are all necessary and useful skills for beginning writers.

Yet our current reading practices and our pedagogies limit more varied and sophisticated readings that take into account our students' diversities. Inquiries into a more flexible space encourage us to think about how we might invite and open more of these spaces in our classrooms to add more depth to our workshops by varying our reading experiences and approaches. If variable interpretive readings are proof that the act of reading is one of creative and active participation rather than passive reception, what pedagogical practices can best help our students to broaden their reader-response awareness and how might they apply new approaches to the ways they approach the writing process? In addition, since creative writing scholarship is still emerging in the field of audience awareness, how might we integrate composition and literary studies theory into our pedagogical practice? To extend this further, how might we learn from these theoretical applications, refine them for our practices, integrate them with our theories of writerly reading and form new reading theories – new course development? This dialogue begins to explore some of these questions by pointing to those practices in place.

Teaching reader-response awareness

Students in introductory creative writing classes have limited to no experience reading as a writer. In fact, the data collected by Colin Irvine (2010), a composition teacher who questions why it is that despite strong pedagogical practices students remain as poor readers, suggest that perhaps there are underlying physiological and cognitive reasons for our students' reading performance. We might explore Irvine's findings as they relate to our creative writing students. Our beginning writing students, for example, demonstrate some cognitive dysfunction when they find it difficult to holistically approach a reading of their peers' work. Despite teacher instructions to consider the whole of a story or poem, students still tend to comment on more surface issues; they become, as Irvine says, 'error hunters' (p. 136). Irvine reports the findings of a technologic study of student eye movements conducted by Eric J. Paulson, Jonathan Alexander and Sonya Armstrong, authors of 'Peer review re-viewed: Investigating the juxtaposition of composition students' eye movements and peer review processes'. This inquiry and analysis demonstrates that 'participants looked at the errors in the essay far more often, and for far longer, than any other word in the essay' (qtd. in Irvine, 2010: 136).

To add to this information, Irvine discovers from post-process theorists Thomas Kent and Donald Davidson that writing (in addition to other communication transactions) is 'largely paralogic in nature rather than systematic' (p. 136). This study affirms the cognitive reports by Fish and Iser that our students approach the text with prior theories of what it might mean, and, as such, 'reading involves a series of learned and highly contextual hermeneutic guesses' (Thomas Kent and Donald Davidson, qtd.

in Irvine, 2010: 137). What complicates this process, and this brings me to the point I want to make here, is that not only do our students' basic reading skills result from a long history of linear reading practices, but they bring to their reading methods certain assumptions, which, for the most part, exist without their conscious awareness. With this is mind, teachers can construct alternative pedagogies that consider and then challenge their students' pre-existing reading skills to help students become more diversified and developed readers.

One such challenge to our students reading practices is to begin by exposing the assumptions, beliefs and expectations that students bring to their readings. For instance, Larry Anderson (1991: 144) addresses two important assumptions with his students when he introduces reader-response theory to his introductory literature class as a way of setting the stage for a new way of reading. The first assumption is that 'there is no such thing as a context-free discourse' (1991: 144). Anderson tells his students, 'rhetoric has always viewed discourse as a social phenomenon; and literature can certainly be seen as such'. His pedagogy follows a basic rhetorical principle: 'To understand discourse one must understand its context' and appreciate that there are always available '[a] variety of forces... always present: historical, sociopolitical, cultural, and situational' (p. 144). His second assumption suggests that there is 'no such thing as random discourse', as '[r]hetoric takes all language to be purposive' (p. 144). He uses the traditional communication triangle to outline the transaction of writer, reader and language.

Although Anderson's pedagogy presents to an introductory literature class, it can very easily be adapted to a creative writing classroom to gain the same results. He distributes a short story to the class (he prefers Washington Irving's 'The stout gentleman') and requests that students read the story and write a reaction to it. He requires only two steps for this assignment: students are to interpret the assignment in writing and explain how certain craft elements (plot, characterization, setting and such) contribute to their reaction. Anderson shares the student responses with the class to demonstrate what kinds of assumptions, expectations and biases they bring to their readings. It is from this platform that he advances the discussion so that students might see the assumptions underlying the surface of their responses. He asks his students 'whether it is possible that the "point" of the story is to *have an effect*. Could we not say this about all stories: do not all texts have effects on their readers?' (p. 143). Here is where Anderson comes close to merging what goes on in the creative writing class and what is possible with reader-response theory.

Anderson comes close – but there is a difference. Once the craft and structure of a story or poem is discussed, creative writers do not necessarily wonder if the point of the story is to have an effect; rather, because we are reading as writers, we consider the writer's choices and how these choices have an effect on our reading – and therein lies the difference. The effect might be related to suspense, credibility, character motivation, complications in plot, increasing stakes and/or shifts in tone or direction to name a few. At this point, students might engage in questions of 'What if?' in their attempt to imagine how a story or poem might be different or can be different at any point. What is missing from this creative writing discussion, that Anderson's pedagogy supplies, is a reader-response perspective. Such a reader-response strategy might intensify students' engagement and open spaces for dialogue that links, layers, conflicts, interacts – or any combination of the above – the reading of a story as a writer and the implications of assumptions and biases that students bring to each text that they read. Additionally, there are opportunities to broaden the possibilities for a story or poem construct when we consider the differing and often conflicting reader responses.

Teaching reader-response strategies

Making creative writing students more aware of reading response is a critical first step in introducing alternative reading practices. Bizzaro's (1993) book *Responding to Student Poems* provides, in addition to useful information on the theories of literary study and the roles of teacher and students, a representation of his reading, commenting and evaluating of students' poems through several applications. Under the heading of 'What teachers should know', Bizzaro addresses the need to 'view revision less as the application of certain rules and procedures to a nearly finished text and more as an effort to unfold meaning in a manner that somehow makes possible a similar unfolding for the reader' (1993: 68). Feedback shifts from the normative New Critical evaluation of the text to one which 'must thus be nonjudgmental and provide the writer with clues as to how the text might better create the envisioned audience' (1993: 68). While the teacher privileges the reader in a reader-response classroom, '[i]nteraction and shared authority are at the center of any method of evaluation and reading founded upon reader-response theories' (1993: 69). Students approach revision differently than they would when the meaning and expression is privileged in the text.

Bizzaro discovers that his students' revisions are more inclined to 'the evolving relationship between the writer and reader as they determine what the text will be' than the text itself (1993: 69). He applies reader-response criticism to student poems by emphasizing the reading and not the text as he makes parallel texts, which reflects his reader reactions alongside student poems. Bizzaro admits to the concerted effort in staying true to this method (not reverting back to traditional readings, assessing for audience, generating questions to the author as to how passages might be read). What he discovers in his reading practice is that though he has used a questioning rather than a directive approach, it is difficult to limit himself to this reader-response perspective. On the premise that readers evoke or invoke a particular audience in their writing (see literary theorist Iser, 1974; and composition theorists Ong, 1975 and Ede & Lunsford, 1988), Bizzaro advises his student-writer as to how well the intended audience has been invoked. As such, he performs 'as a writerly reader in reconstructing the text' (1993: 71).

What is equally appreciated in this pedagogical model are Bizzaro's honest comments as he struggles with false starts, shifts in authority and questions of teaching effectiveness. In the end, he comes to appreciate the shared power and the legitimacy of the reader response. Revisions of student poems based on his reader-response feedback tended to be more extensive and Bizzaro reports that this receptive reading allowed him to provide the author with more commentary. Reader-response models give teachers the courage to change and supplement reading strategies.

While there is value in exploring the reader-response model in the creative writing classroom, there is benefit to having students approach reading from variable perspectives and lenses (e.g. Feminist, New Criticism, Deconstruction and others) to best appreciate reading strategies as well as to decenter other less useful strategies. A course that teaches the reading and writing of these strategies would be productive for creative writing students.

Finally, the extent by which digital production has changed the way we read texts, impacts the role of audience in entirely different ways than print production does. In 'The meanings of "audience"', Douglas Park (1982: 249) addresses the divergence of the meanings of audience in two general directions: 'one toward actual people external to a text', which he refers to as 'the audience whom the writer must accommodate', and 'the other toward the text itself and the audience implied there'. In the first case, the audience may be readers of a particular genre, and in the case of the second, the audience might be implied through 'a set of suggested or evoked attitudes, interests, reactions, conditions of knowledge which may or may not fit with the qualities of actual readers' (p. 249). As options for our students' writing expression increase through digital platforms, writers now create poems and stories and hybrids of both genres with the technology of new media in mind, and, as such, writing in public spaces with all of its multimodal textuality complicates the concept of audience and reader-response.

Social Relations: Through a Lacanian Lens

When meaning lies with the reader in the communication transaction, the students' Symbolic order comes into play. If we follow the assumptions of the reader-response theory, then we see the reader as the one who projects her self-understanding, her culturally determined assumptions when she interacts with the text. She shapes the text and, as Fish claims, the text functions as a mirror that provides the reader's reflection. The hermeneutical circle creates for the reader a circuitous route in which the reader seeks constituted representations of herself as much as that is possible. When a teacher's pedagogy privileges meaning in the reader she situates herself as a welcomed reader, one who shares authority with the writer and other model readers.

This pedagogical approach is likely the most symbiotic of the practices discussed for several reasons. First, if we follow Lacan's theory of transference, then the 'divided self', which represents the student on one side of the mirror, looks to the teacher as the one who *supposes to know*. The teacher represents, in Lacanian psychology, the other half of the divided self – figuratively, a student's mirrored reflection. In order for there to be a positive transference, which enables learning to take place, the student waits for the teacher to provide her with the answers as the student believes the teacher is supposed to know. The instructor, to best facilitate this positive transference, asks questions as a 'model reader' might. As a result, the student does not get the quick answer she expects, and thus must search for answers on her own. Her search brings her to answers and learning takes place. In the end, the student 'trusts' the teacher, and transference is positive.

The important relationship then is within the divided person (her conscious self and her image of the teacher as the one who knows best). To this end, transferring an image of the self onto the analyst, the 'divided' person finds in the Symbolic Other (the *Subject Supposed to Know*) an external means to express his or her inner dialogue. Moreover, it might be conjectured that since Fish perceives the text as a mirror for the reader, that the text, in a sense, reflects the reader's image. It seems plausible that in Lacanian terms, there would be, in this context, implications of 'divided self' and identity.

Reader-Response Theory: Final Arguments

Jane Tompkins (1980: 201) presents an interesting perspective that positions the reader-response theory as one that parallels the formalist reading of New Criticism in which the object of study is the text. She argues that '[t]he essential similarity between New Criticism and reader-response criticism is obscured by the great issue that seems to divide them: whether meaning is to be located in the text or in the reader' (p. 206). While both critics locate meaning in different places, Tompkins' argument rests on the impression (which she deems faulty) that 'the specification of meaning is the aim of the critical act' (p. 206). [As such, meaning as the aim of the critical act, 'binds [Reader-Response theory and New Criticism] together in opposition to a long history of critical thought in which the specification of meaning is not a central concern' (p. 206).

Her argument comes from a hierarchal assessment of what constitutes a justifiable aim in the critical act. More specifically, when the preferred study of literature is interpretive, critics of literary studies measure other approaches to the study of literature as having less value. In other words, determining where meaning lies in the composing process (whether in New Criticism or reader-response theories) is not as significant as the interpretive deconstruction of a text.

If reading a student's text suggests that the meaning of a text is in the hands of the reader, then teachers risk misinterpreting their students' intended audience. To effectively apply reader-response theory in the creative writing classroom, students should more consciously 'determine who they want their texts to address' (Bizzaro, 1993: 67), and teachers, if they are to help their students keep this audience in mind, will need to 'relinquish some power in examining those texts' (Bizzaro, 1993: 67). Reader-response methods ask teachers (and workshop readers) to read students' work through the lens of the intended reader. If the reading of a student text is approached from a reader-response perspective, then student revision efforts should result in those discoveries that might help the writer to make her text read more as she had intended.

While the four major teaching approaches in the creative writing classroom are discussed in this section, our practices are also informed by a variety of other theorists. From process theorists, we appreciate the recursive nature of writing and the practice of writing. From genre-theory, we value analyzing discourse conventions, applications and genres. From postmodernism, we view the world as text. Writers employ variable lenses in the development of their characters, settings, and scenes. From critical theory, we broaden our canon and better understand language practices as cultural. From collaborative theory, we operate our classrooms as writing communities and join the larger conversations within the field through our national conferences and scholarship. In the area of gender studies (feminist theory, queer theory) we theorize on a more equitable society and challenge writing/reading in a dominant discourse. From technorhetoricians, we engage in new writing spaces, creating stories and poems in multimodal forms. From assessment theory, we strive to identify our benchmarks of measurements and revisit our student outcomes and program design. All of these theoretical frameworks suggest useful critical positions from which to explore the ways in which we position meaning in our teaching practice.

Notes

1. This discussion of ways to move beyond New Critic reading and writing in the creative writing classroom is also discussed in my essay 'Creative writing and composition: Re-writing the lines' in the P. Bizzaro et al. (eds.) 2011c pedagogy book that honors Wendy Bishop.
2. The Inspiration Approach to teaching is further discussed by Hal Blythe and Charlie Sweet in 'The writing community: A new model for the creative writing classroom'. *Pedagogy* 8 (2), 305–325.
3. See http://www.uiowa.edu/~iww/about.htm

SECTION 2

The Writing Workshop Model

A Workshop Survey

Defining the Workshop Model

A Study of the Workshop Model

How Our Workshop History Informs Our Praxes

Perceptions and Practice

Developing Markers of Professional Difference

The Case for Creative Writing Research as Knowledge

The Workshop Model: Final Arguments

The Writing Workshop Model

Those of us in creative writing must, *if* we are to move beyond questions of whether the workshop model works or does not work – or to ask instead more utilitarian questions such as the one Mary Ann Cain (2010: 216) aptly interrogates: 'What makes it possible for those in the academe to keep asking, *'Does it work?'* without any real challenge or inquiry to the question itself' – come to better visualize what *else* is possible in this workshop space. Creative writers have answered the challenge generated by some (Ostrom, Ritter, Vanderslice, Bizzaro, Mayers) of whose interests are served by the replication of the workshop model.[1]

Many agree, as Mayers (2007: 8–9) suggests, that as teachers we are implicated in this answer. Such reproduction can be found in:

- 'creative writing's investment in the notion that writers are born and not made [which] makes the whole issue of pedagogy suspect from the onset';
- the replication of the model by tradition – the 'basically unrevised' model as taught by our mentors;
- our 'lack of explicit attention to pedagogy ... creative writers [who] consider themselves writers who teach, rather than teachers who write';
- the identity of authors as writers first, teachers second; and
- our embracing of the Associated Writing Program's (AWP) version of our identity.

Randall Albers (Columbia College Chicago)[2] validates a couple of these points when he proposes that 'teachers must totally rethink the way they approach the teaching of writing'. He addresses the time and effort this would take, and suggests 'many, many writing teachers are content to do what they were themselves taught'. He submits faculty 'would rather spend that time writing their own work than taking on the extra reading, thinking, experimentation, and training that new models would take'. Rationales for reproducing the workshop from program to program and laying claim to its workability often edify or rouse those in the field, usually without much constructive forward movement or change. Rather than idle over the question of why creative writing teachers continue to hold fast to the traditional workshop model or whether creative writing can be taught, we need to ask instead: What might be gained by flexing the elasticity of the workshop model? How might we add texture and rigor to its applaudable merits? In what ways can markers of professionalism in the workshop model set us apart in our scholarship from composition studies and literary studies?

My inquiry and research of the writing workshop along with my proposal for a more robust and intelligent model are part of an overarching goal to establish *creative writing studies* as an academic discipline. This study suggests that although the model remains dominant in the discipline's field of practice, there is little agreement as to what constitutes the workshop practice in creative writing classrooms across the nation. My research also reveals that more and more teachers are in fact exploring new spaces for the workshop model. I propose that there is significant interest in more radical openness and re-envisioning of the workshop model to warrant a call for further pedagogical inquiry. The hope is that this text and those that follow would be helpful to the field of *creative writing studies*, the profession and our creative writing students.

A Workshop Survey

While there exists some MFA and PhD students who may turn a 'tin ear' to peer responses after too many workshops taken at the undergraduate and graduate level and while the same students may tend to create stories and/or poems that are workshop-ready (too polished) or suited for workshop approval (too safe) or customized for a teacher's preference (too similar in style), the writing workshop model for the most part, especially at the undergraduate level as problematic as it may be, is still the heart of the creative writing program and the favorite part of the course.

My recent survey of undergraduate creative writing teachers at programs predominantly across the United States, my own personal experience as a creative writing teacher and scholarship in creative writing pedagogy inform the basis of my analysis of the workshop. Of the survey, my driving questions prompted responses (to name a few) on the utility of the workshop, its effectiveness and value and its best practices. Respondents considered student motivations, preparedness and readiness for the workshop model. Creative writing teachers offered ways to keep the workshop fresh and alive or they lamented at such futileness. Still others shared exciting corollaries to the model in the classroom. One hundred and sixty-seven creative writing teachers replied to my inquiry (five more participated in an initial test collection) from a base of 174 undergraduate creative writing programs (identified for the most part from the Associated Writing Program's database). While teacher response could be anonymous, 105 did identify their comments and *this* 62% represents a total of 70 colleges and universities.

According to the survey results, nearly 51% of the teachers use a model that is similar to the basic workshop (very *broadly* sketched here as a forum for sharing and commenting on stories and poems by teacher and student readers; with varying rules of operation, the most prominent being the silence of the author during the peer review process) while 39.2% practice a variation of the mode of instruction, and only 10% define their model to be markedly different than the traditional workshop. The model serves as the primary focus or a major component in 80% of creative writing classes. Students can take the workshop-based course as a creative writing requirement (84.9%), as an elective (86.1%), as a writing intensive requirement (35.5%) or for other reasons (enjoyment, outlet for self-expression, general education requirement and such 32.5%), and in some cases students can participate in a workshop course to satisfy more than one requirement at the same time. A majority of institutions (60%) do not require prerequisites or a writing sample/portfolio prior to course enrollment, and 24% of programs call for students to complete a previous semester or two of composition. For the most part, creative writing majors take 15 or more workshop hours in the course of their study.

Overall, the survey demonstrates that creative writing programs still rely on the tradition of the workshop. It remains, as Edward Delaney says, 'the hub of the wheel' (Delaney, 2007). Nancy McCabe (University of Virginia) who has been teaching writing for the past 23 years claims what we all know to be true: 'students always say on evaluations that the workshop portion of the class was the most enjoyable part'. Karl Elder (Lakeland College) concurs, that his class is 'almost universally motivated' by the workshop encounter, and this observation has been my experience as well. Perhaps the basis for why the model retains its place at the center of the creative writing classroom is as Phillip Gross (2010: 52) says, 'a workshop is a very human situation'. Or maybe, when all the spark plugs are firing in sync (or synapses, as the case may be), there is nowhere else in academia where students can 'find a rigorous program of study that is also directly personal for them' (Lisa Roney, University of Central Florida).

It might hold true that some of us will follow the logic of polemics put forward in Michelene Wandor's (2008) *The Author is Not Dead, Merely*

Somewhere Else, Dana Gioia's (1991) *Atlantic Monthly* essay 'Can poetry matter?', Donald Hall's (1988) 'Poetry and ambition' or its short story counterpart written by John Aldridge (1990) 'The assembly-line fiction', and John Barr's (2006) 'American poetry in the new century'. In these argumentations, the workshop is either stripped of any rational or purposeful function or the type of writing generated from workshops reportedly has no readership outside the academia. The complaint is that creative writing programs have yet to produce another Mark Twain, Walt Whitman or Emily Dickinson. What is more, we might find disheartening the renouncements by those in the field such as poet and critic Allen Tate (1964), who also ran the creative writing program at Princeton. Tate complains about the sameness of teaching modalities, the workshop implied in his argument, noting that 'the academically certified Creative Writer goes out to teach Creative Writing, and produces other Creative Writers who are not writers, but who produce still other Creative Writers who are not writers' (p. 181). Similarly, Kay Boyle, though a teacher for 16 years at the San Francisco State creative writing program, suggests, '[a]ll creative-writing programs ought to be abolished by law' (qtd. in Menand, 2009). Some may be familiar with R.V. Cassill's response at a Boston convention, ironically, on the 15th anniversary of the Associated Writers Program (now called the Association of Writers & Writing Programs) to disband the very organization he founded in 1967. In this address, Cassill derided the complacency of writers, the corruptness of the academic system and the poisoning by departments and institutions. It was time for writers, he insisted, to get out of the university (Menand, 2009).

It is hard to dismiss, offhandedly, such cancellations of support by those who have respectable histories like Cassill. He is writer, critic, author of the popular textbook *Writing Fiction*, teacher at Brown University and the original editor of *The Norton Anthology of Short Fiction*. Still, despite apologias that shake the workshop at its core, some of us may murmur from a position *sans* theory, *sans* standards, *sans* empirical data, 'like Galileo at his inquisition', like Philip Gross (2010: 52) of Glamorgan University: *'Eppur si Muove*. And yet it moves'.

Defining the Workshop Model

When one speaks of the pedagogy or the discipline of creative writing, the workshop is implied in the address. The model might be defined as 'competent but uncompelling' (Myers, 1996: 118) or as a place where we 'teach craft and discourage self-indulgent junk' (Toni Graham, OK State). Philip Roth contends the workshop serves three objectives: 'to give young writers an audience, a sense of community, and an acceptable social category – student' (qtd. in Grimes, 1999: 4). Anna Leahy (2010: 62) views teaching as a creative act, and understands the workshop 'as an overarching pedagogical outlook and learning environment', one which offers 'community' as a critical element 'for creative production' (p. 67). She sees the workshop as 'good' for the profession and for students, noting that the pedagogy 'is supported by cognitive science as well as the craft criticism of writers themselves' (p. 67). Our goals for our undergraduates may be lofty as we wish to 'enhance students' understanding of the meaning of art in their lives' (Karl Elder, Lakeland College) or far-reaching as we strive 'to create deeper, closer, more responsible and creative thinkers, readers, and writers' (Lisa Russ Spaar, University of Virginia). Michelene Wandor (2008: 124) likens what we do in the workshop model to the 'academic practice of peer-reviewing (in journals and publishing)'. Peter Harris (Colby College) finds the space 'a wonderful place where people's lives open up', where they 'begin to own their own voices'. The pedagogy introduces vocabulary necessary for the discussion of texts. It also foregrounds writing as process.

For most, the operation of the model often depends on course level and teacher design. Some teachers approach the workshop with a heavy reading list such as the instructor whose workshop syllabus requires students to read 10 books over the course of the semester or the one who assigns long, difficult novels. There are those who view the workshop as a course in craft, a study in how to read poetry, how to identify elements of fiction, how to appreciate the choices writers make, how to imagine ways in which these choices might have been different; how to – as Martin Cockroft of Waynesburg University suggests – 'reform student ideas about what *is* poetry, what is possible in the form, and how it can/ought to be written'. In still other classes, the students' work is the center of the course; the workshop functions as the single pedagogy. Some teachers support the practice of free-writing, others prefer invention strategies such as exercises and writing prompts to generate story and poem seeds. For the instructors at Columbia Chicago College, the model differs from the traditional one in that theirs is a process-based story workshop, one that uses 'classic, storytelling forms, along with skills of conceptualizing, abstracting, critical thinking, and imaginative problem-solving' to supplement basic skills (Randall Albers). Most would agree with Sue Roe (2010: 204), who claims: 'Workshops are fundamental – launch pads rather than flights, rehearsal strategies rather than the exigencies of polished and finessed performance'. Some might also agree with Maurice Guevara (1998) that its design can be 'sin of all sins – unimaginative'.

A Study of the Workshop Model

Before undertaking a defense of a rigorous writing workshop it is important to outline a more global assertion on behalf of creative writing as an academic discipline. Briefly restated, in order for creative writing to advance as an academic discipline in its own right, it must undergo an inquiry into its field, much like composition studies did in the middle to late 20th century. This field of inquiry, a factor critical to the development of *creative writing studies*, necessarily explores the pedagogical problems and paradoxes of the discipline. Such internal complexities are typically the impetus that sets a programmatic evolution in motion of which *creative writing studies* is situated in its early phase. Ritter and Vanderslice (2007: xv) remind us that 'a field whose teaching practices and theories are relatively unexamined runs the risk of being dominated by an ever more unwieldy body of knowledge and practices, some of which have likely outgrown their usefulness or been misapplied'.

The workshop, as the default model of pedagogy in creative writing classrooms, has been, Bizzaro (2004: 296) says, our 'model of instruction [for] over a hundred years', and as Peter Vandenberg (2004: 7) infers, our practice 'is ripe for annexation'. Consider that AWP's 2010 *Guide to Writing Programs* points to a significant rise in creative writing programs. The 79 undergraduate and graduate creative writing programs recorded in 1975 pales to the reported present figure of 822. Of this number, more than 300 are at the graduate level (37 award the PhD), and thousands of students are enrolled nationally (AWP website, 2010). Now consider that every program, according to Virginia's Christopher Tilghman, 'devotes 50 percent of its time to the workshop' (qtd. in Delaney, 2007). Given these staggering statistics, the workshop's universality, its application at all levels to vitally diverse populations, its differing teacher foci, and its reportedly mixed results, in the words of Hans Ostrom (1994: xix–xx), 'all of us could probably benefit from taking a hard look at precisely how "the workshop" functions in our classrooms'. Such an inquiry asks us to consider at a microcosmic level:

> [W]hat are our guidelines, and what assumptions underlie them? How explicitly do we probe the criteria for assessing work-in-progress? What is our role in workshops and group work, and how productive has this role been? What other roles might we experiment with? What else should go on in a workshop besides the workshop? To what extent are we 'playing the old tapes' of workshops we took? What do we know about group dynamics, and what should we know? Who gets silenced

in our workshops and why? How often do we/should we revise our workshop methods? When are the conversations in our workshops most productive and why? What might be gained by dismantling the workshop model altogether and starting from scratch? (Ostrom, 1994: xix–xx)

On a more macrocosmic grade, if *creative writing studies* is to operate as a more distinct academic discipline, then scholarship at a curricular level should, as Haake suggests, 'seek to move beyond our preoccupation with the writer or the text to the role of creative writing as an academic discipline inside a profession that includes, but is not limited to, the production and teaching of imaginative writing' (qtd. in Mayers, 2009: 218). Vanderslice (2010: 35) tells us that the workshop 'can be rescued from the moving stream that threatens to carry it into iconoclastic oblivion, and recast, recreated into something lithe and supple'. This 're-casting' begins with establishing 'markers of professional difference' (Ritter, 2001: 208) to include ways in which the field of creative writing is set apart in its scholarship from other work of English studies. These are significant undertakings, and yet, as Bizzaro (1998: 287) 'envisions there may be a great many teachers of creative writing like himself' interested in discussing and debating pedagogy. I wish to join that discussion and debate by continuing the field's inquiry and offering not a dismantling of the workshop model or even a simple re-tooling (which would not address more systemic issues),[3] but rather a more enlightened view of the model as an intelligent and robust pedagogy, one we might advance with our emergent field of *creative writing studies*.

Dawson's question – 'Is the pedagogical process merely guided by idiosyncrasies of each teacher, the practicing writer able to pass on knowledge by virtue of his or her innate talent and secret knowledge of the craft?' (qtd. in Ritter & Vanderslice, 2007: xiii) – is more than rhetorical, and it has merit when we consider that the workshop model offers no real standards of measurement. Bizzaro (2004: 295) reminds us that we have practiced this 'basically unrevised' century-old method 'without giving it proper scrutiny'. Sharing stories and poems, reading from a writerly perspective, providing helpful feedback, re-envisioning works-in-progress, are at least some of the functions of the traditional workshop model. Its practice has become so deeply-ingrained in our pedagogy that it continues without question. Or if it *is* questioned – in the sense that many of us are uneasy with varying degrees of a workshop's artificiality, ethical disparities, multiversity, idleness, singularity, program design, authority, evaluation, absence of theory and/or its range of student readiness, preparedness and motivation – we are at a loss as to how to fix it.

If what seems to be a melting pot approach to the model boils down to a little of this and a lot of that, a community crock pot of flavors, it is no wonder that, at times, we are unsure of just what it is we taste in this covered dish – this workshop. And we wonder, how might it sustain us?

For instance, we may suggest that as untrained creative writers, we are teaching 'by the seat of our pants', our workshops presumably 'unstructured and friendly' (Leahy, 2005: 20). This relaxed, we're-just-chatting consciousness surfaces regardless of how much planning goes into the class. Others could suggest we operate our workshops in a vacuum, with a separatist view that defers outside reference; certainly, AWP's mission statement supports this position. Gross (2010: 54) reminds us that the workshop 'is not a *thing*', but rather 'a group of people brought together in a time and place'; it involves a human experience. Graeme Harper (2010: xv) emphasizes that the workshop relates to 'things we do' instead of 'the objects we made', and Gaylene Perry (2010: 118) concurs that 'the act of writing is a highly physical one, complete with its own dynamics and energy' – energy, she tells us, 'that must not be wasted – because it precipitates rich moments of teaching and learning'. A workshop does not enact one *'game'*, Gross insists, one 'set of conventions', but rather a workshop 'is the conventions that shape what participants expect' (p. 55). The majority opinion is that we practice the workshop model as our primary pedagogy, sometimes emulating our own mentors because these are the methods from which we have learned. Or perhaps, the workshop 'has remained', as Haake (2010: 182) says, 'as close to a home as we are ever going to come in the academy'. Even with this thought, the one thing Haake and many of us can say with any certainty about the workshop remains, 'that's not it, that's still not it' (2010: 182).

To illustrate this patchwork of practices, we could consider some workshop praxes and teacher perspectives. For example, if one teacher supports, encourages even, personal self-discovery (and recovery?) and another endorses the objectification of the text, excluding all outside factors; and the instructor in the neighboring academy focuses mostly on writerly techniques found within the current *Best American Short Stories* with a portion of the class dedicated to writing activities, and if a creative writing teacher in rural Idaho sanctions the bulk of classroom time to the critique of students' texts, and if the instructor who teaches inner city students refuses to abide by the author gag rule of the traditional workshop because her students' voices have been silenced long enough, then how can the writing workshop be contained within the same pedagogical model?

How in fact can it not be paradoxical in nature or contradictory in its aims? Michelene Wandor (2010: 128) addresses such antipathetic purposes when she says:

> [I]f creative writing is training professional writers (those who already have 'talent'), then the great-writers approach privileges the text over the writer; if students are taught that creative writing expresses the self (writing as therapy), then the person is privileged over the writing. The first overvalues the art, the second overvalues the person, and together they confuse the object of the work and its objectives.

To add to this, there are inconsistent issues related to an egalitarian relationship when both teacher and student assume the role of 'writer'. For instance, Mayers (2007: 4) references the pronged '[e]litist versus democratic' scenario: democratic in the sense that 'newcomers might make significant contributions' to literature and elitist in 'identifying in the end only a select few students who might be worthy of the label "real writer"'. Additionally, the 'theoretical egalitarian responses of the peer friendly' workshop create an addling for our students when the postscript to their default response of praise contradicts that of the teacher (known as a 'tutor' in the United Kingdom) who has ultimate authority as evaluator of students' work upon completion of the course (Wandor, 2008: 127). These built-in tensions are reflected in Siobhan Holland's collective response of some of the delegates at the 2001 creative writing conference at the Bath Spa University. Holland argues, '[i]t is not fair to students to find their work praised in workshops and criticised in [tutor] assessment feedback' (qtd. in Wandor, 2008: 127). What is more, an ethical dilemma presents when we are faced with the decision to silence the author and her valued intentions and processes versus justifying this traditional silence as a necessary function of minimizing the writer's defense and maximizing her processing of the workshop response. Complicating these paradoxes are the ethics of exposing personal experience in the workshop and the standard of measurements for such writing reflection. What goes on in a workshop can be '*outrageous, ethically questionable, new, ugly, badly untheorized, awkward... embarrassing, messy, inarticulate, ineloquent, astonishing, and explosive*' (Perry, 2010: 117, author's italics). The 'potentially dangerous' function of the workshop is, Perry (2010: 128) insists, 'crucial to the workshop's success' because '[t]he vulnerability involved in creativity is what feeds and energises it' (2010: 128). Finally, though the list of ambiguities may go on, the traditional workshop may move along the 'consensus' principles of Kenneth Bruffee's (1984) collaborative learning theory. It may also butt against 'dissensus' as argued by those like compositionist John Trimbur (1989).

Granted, the workshop is a 'process' and, as such, its 'plasticity' conforms to individual manipulation, and its response depends to some degree on the dynamics and preparedness of each particular class. However, if we continue to place such emphasis on the workshop *process* in our classrooms, if we name it our 'practice', our 'signature pedagogy', if we assign it curricular substance for fulfillment of a degree and usher our students out into the workforce and community with diploma in hand, then should we not consider how we manage that which defines the heart of our course?

More importantly, given such variances within our pedagogy, how can the workshop *be* properly scrutinized? If we were in fact to examine it in such regard, how might we determine what happens in the workshop and why? To ask the enveloping question then: how are we to evaluate if the writing workshop model still works? By extension, as it is implicated in the workability of the model, when many question whether creative writing can be taught, and if so how is it taught, and who can teach it – questions, by the way, which have been asked long before the new compositionists embodied a constructivist view that 'genius', 'imagination' and 'power' were not given but obtainable – is it enough then when someone like Mark Winegardner of Florida State counters with 'You can't teach every piano player to be Thelonious Monk, but no piano teacher seems tortured by the question of whether piano can be *taught*'? (qtd. in Healey, 2009). Is it enough to say, as John Barth did in a 1985 article in *The New York Times Book Review* titled 'Writing: Can it be taught?', that 'emphatically it can, mainly on the ground that it so emphatically *is*'? (qtd. in Menand, 2009, my emphasis). Where might one begin this ontological study? The answers to probing questions such as these are, as Shirley Geok-lin Lim (2003: 157) notes in her essay 'The strangeness of creative writing', 'so nuanced, constrained, interrogated, and indeterminable as to raise more questions'. Indeed, I say.

Part of the difficulty in even defining the workshop, let alone reconceptualizing it as a rigorous and intelligent pedagogy, relates to the elasticity of the model – its ability to morph into variable shapes, to stretch in so many ways and, as such, it is easy, like Saran wrap, to take it for granted. My goal is not to dismiss variances of the workshop model, but rather I want to explore current practices of creative writing's signature pedagogy as part of an overarching inquiry into the field with a secondary goal to help *creative writing studies* ascend as a distinct discipline independent in its own scholarship.

How Our Workshop History Informs Our Praxes

Prior to the conception of the Iowa-based academic workshop model, writing colonies gathered outside of institutions in such places as Nashville, Iowa City and Greenwich Village as a pre-war rebellion against restrictive university curriculums. These writing clubs created spaces where students and faculty could share their work and receive criticism. In addition, writers such as 'Frost, Sandburg, Dreiser, Mencken, Stephen Crane, Sinclair Lewis, and Hemingway held jobs as cub reporters, learning about factual narrative and detailed observation, a training that influenced the form of the modern novel' (Adams, 1993: 90–91). These influences are worth mentioning because by the 1920s, much of this off-campus tradition moved onto campus and along with it came its writers, who were given, more often than not, favorable positions that accounted for their first priority: their writing life. For example, historian Katherine Adams (1993: 93) in *A History of Professional Writing Instruction in American Colleges* notes that a writer-in-residence position offered to playwright Percy MacKaye at Miami University of Ohio in 1920 also included 'building him a much-publicized studio and requiring him to perform few academic duties'. The same relaxed instructional responsibilities held true for Robert Frost as poet-in-residence at the University of Michigan during 1921–1922 (Adams, 1993: 93), and many more examples followed. Today, the great writers' approach still occurs at many of the top programs. These writers 'teach infrequently (one class in a year or year and a half seems typical) because their published works are believed to do more than their teaching for the program's image. This is because writing programs must contend with the authorial "star system"' (qtd. in Delaney, 2007). Such hiring expenses and star system adulations, cycle the university perception (which then cycle such beliefs at the program, student and community level) that only notable writers who are well-published with prestigious presses can teach creative writers.

Even before the onset of post-war second-generation teachers and the 'elephant machine' replication of the workshop pedagogy – a metaphorical vehicle for the production of other writers and other workshops as referenced in Myers' (1996) *The Elephants Teach* – writers brought a less-than-academic focus to the creative writing classroom. Their emphasis was on student manuscripts, not on required readings or craft discussions or creative exercises and assignments as they are in current conventions. Pulitzer Prize poets such as Robert Frost and Richard Wilbur would never have considered creative practice or writing prompts in their workshop settings. In fact Wilbur insists, 'I don't want to turn my students into clever executors of formal problems. I want them to start the way any kind of poet starts, with the matter, with the urge ...' (qtd. in Garrett, 1989: 94). The preferred style of these writer-teachers was similar to critique sessions like those the Fugitives held in Nashville (Adams, 1993: 93). Some continue this argument today when they say that the contemporary workshop model has little value or basis for authentic learning. Grant Matthew Jenkins (University of Tulsa), for instance, steers clear of the artificiality of the workshop model. Instead, he attempts to recreate for his students the life and work of poets like himself and others. He states:

> I don't sit around with my poet friends and critique their work. Instead, we read seminal works about relevant issues ... collaborate on projects, host readings, give each other poems (as gifts but sometimes for comment), buy each other's books, solicit manuscripts, invite each other to readings, etc. This experiential mode gives students a much better view of the life of a poet than the arbitrary and artificial workshop model.

Similarly, one teacher, responding to my survey, agrees that 'learning' to 'improve your writing' cannot 'be communicated in a classroom; or, for that matter, between two writers, no matter how well-intentioned'. S/he urges that 'learning how to write in a voice that's your own isn't found that way, and, despite the forests of rubbish written on the subject, there isn't a good writer alive who won't tell you the same thing'. This instructor also advises, '[i]t's living you have to do more of, not workshopping, in order to become a writer'.

To return to the workshop history: prior to the war, early orchestration of the academic workshop began in Harvard's advanced creative composition classes followed by a Verse Making course at Iowa in 1897 and a drama graduate workshop course at Harvard from 1906 to 1925. Norman Foerster, director of the Iowa School of Letters from 1930 to 1944, was successful in implementing the creative dissertation in the PhD curriculum, a program meant to include a creative and critical study for all English-majoring students. The 'workshop' launched in 1936 under the direction of William Schramm as did the awarding of the MFA degree in creative writing. In succeeding Schramm and Foerster, Paul Engle dropped the critical component of creative writing study and focused instead on the studio-based workshop model in the 1940s and 1950s, the same model which would, in effect, become the archetype for creative writing courses. In 1949, an undergraduate workshop-based creative writing program was offered as an English major. Because the method was intended for the teaching of graduate students, it would soon prove troubling for instructors who imported it into their undergraduate classes.

Creative writing's original goal to teach writing for its own sake changed with the university's expansion of its role in society and its institutional sanctuary for the arts. It is here where creative writing essentially splits from literary studies in terms of its influence on a writer's education in criticism. At this point, creative writing becomes subject to patronage and growth within the institution. The post-war expansion encouraged an influx of returning veterans onto college campuses (Louis Menand in a recent *New Yorker* article reports this number to be greater than 2 million) and, more specifically, into writing workshops by way of the G.I. Bill. The Bill stipulated that tuition assistance could only be applied to degree or certificate programs, and this directive was the impetus for the development of degree-granting creative writing programs.

This student demographic was less interested in studying the Classics or the British literary canon, demanding instead a more relevant study of literature (T.S. Eliot, W.B. Yeats, Faulkner, Fitzgerald). At this point, universities (aside from their purist literature professors) were more amenable to new courses and modern literature. The Iowa Workshop took on a militaristic atmosphere, one that simulated the boot camp environment familiar to this predominantly male population. As such, workshop critiques were brutal, derisive, gruff – delivered for the purpose of shaping the 'talented' writer and his work for the hard-core reception of editors and publishers. Although I do not intend to be inclusive, for the most part workshop atmospheres today range from this similar battleful mode – that drives 'our need for absolution', and our students to 'taste something fetid at the back of their mouths which won't dissolve no matter how many times they spit' (Domina, 1994: 27) – to a workshop ethos that is much more polite, to an expressive theory of permitting which is analogous to those theories underpinning progressive education, to Romantic outlets for self-discovery and stalwarts for inspiration, to ignoring the author in our objectifications of the text, to an audience-invoked/evoked reception, to something entirely different or a combination of the above. Creative writing's new post-war goal became the production of teachers, an ambition clearly evidenced by the proliferation of workshop-based programs founded mostly by Iowa Workshop graduates in the sixties. 'Between 1960 and 1969, enrollments doubled', Menand (2009) tells us, and 'more professors were hired than had been hired in the entire previous three hundred and twenty-five years'. This coincides with Sharon O'Dair's (2000: 46) account in 'Stars, tenure, and the death of ambition' that – in general – 'life was far less rigorous and competitive' for graduate students and junior English department faculty during the fifties and sixties. George Levine (1993: 45) points to his own hiring experience as an example by noting, '[w]e were less troubled ... at the very moment when English and higher education were experiencing their most rapid and rich expansions ever'. It was not unusual, he continues, for most of his colleagues to receive 'at least three job offers'. Today, more than 2000 graduate students in the United States compete for the approximately 100 tenure-track faculty jobs in creative writing (Menand, 2009). In the sixties, colleges and universities became patrons of writers' careers, and the NEA, established in 1965, would add to this patronage, allocating funds to writers in the university, to literary publishers and to venues for readings and residencies.

As alumni of the workshop-based programs received publication notoriety, universities, in turn, received endowments in part because of their teachers' writing prestige, which, in turn, drew student interest, increased enrollment and opportunities for further expansion. Professionalization through the AWP led to curriculum guidelines and support of the MFA degree as the appropriate credential for the teacher of creative writing. The workshop model was considered as the preferred venue of study. Our 21st century scenario is quite different in that many hiring colleges and universities, offering tenure-track positions, often sidestep the MFA graduate in their preference for the PhD-degreed applicant although experience and publication history still prevail as hiring requisites.

With the graduation of veterans in the early 1950s, there came a change, George Garrett (1989: 50) remarks, 'from the hard experience of the veterans ... to the younger students who lacked this same maturity'. In addition, a shift 'from content, in terms of importance, to form' occurred (p. 50). Garrett, who experienced this transition first-hand, reports that students were now reading *The Catcher in the Rye* and *Lord of the Flies*. He speaks of the mounting dissent between literary studies and creative writing as the 'Beat Movement', formed by 'mildly disgruntled academics' who began to balk at theory and 'fight over the canon' (p. 50). For the poets, literary study had 'no point of contact with concerns of most working poets', and the critics discarded the workshop's production of poems and stories as 'pseudo-lit' (Garrett, 1989: 50). These perspectives add to the split between creative writing and criticism and the ensuing isolationism and marginalization of creative writers and creative writing programs.

In going forward from this point, I'll touch on some of the more significant approaches and their consequential effects on today's workshop praxes. In the sixties and seventies, expressivist views placed the writer at the center of the rhetorical triangle, promoting a sense of the writer, a presence of 'voice' in student writing. This practice continues today as many creative writing teachers place the writer at the center of the workshop, fostering the discovery of a student's voice. Expressivists had no use for theorists or anything that might divert the attention from students or teaching. We see this atheoretical stance in our contemporary workshop-based classrooms as creative writing teachers form the 'disproportionate share of those who retreat from theory' (Ostrom, 1994: xii).

Cognitive process theorists and social constructionists challenged the expressivist view in the eighties, cognitivists first with their study of writing processes. Bizzaro (Bizzaro & McClanahan, 2007: 81) reminds us that '[t]hose who argue for the influence of culture on the development of individual identity – *social constructionists* or *social epistemics* – argue that there is no such thing as an autonomous self'. 'As a result', he notes, 'teaching that was intended to produce voice was off target, wrong in its assumptions about writers, who they are and what they do' (2007: 81). In the eighties, the teacher who supports expressivism in the classroom was felt to play a passive role, failing to provide structure, conventions and strategies. Expressivist rhetoric – and this includes the rhetoric in poetry and fiction, according to James Berlin (1987a), leader of the anti-expressivist campaign – hopes to promote individualism. Expressivist rhetoric also ignores economic, social and political conditions, and can marginalize people who resist, thus empowering them through isolation. Bizzaro (Bizzaro & McClanahan, 2007: 81) suggests that '[c]reative writers and teachers of creative writing did not know (and many still do not know) that they were the ones being spoken to and about'. While the workshop goal of helping students find their own *voice* continues both in the traditional sense of self-expression and in new ways as it relates to challenging assumptions and master narratives, Greg Light (1999) offers an enlightening 'conception of learning' as it relates to *voice*, pinpointing the description of voice as coming from the personal self. Rather, he suggests that '*voice* is better understood in terms of the writer's *conception* of the practice of writing'. In this context voice is not 'authentic' or 'inauthentic' so much as 'integrated' or 'detached'. As such it is not simply a function of the writer 'but of the socio-cultural situation in which the writer is writing' (p. 13).

To continue, there are other historical markers that still affect the workshop model. Ostrom contends that those influenced by postmodern theory 'appear to cut the writer loose from all moorings, sanctioning an anything-goes classroom' (1994: xv). He refers to these groupings as 'elite guilds who rush ahead of the novice theorist, wagging fingers. Novices are sure they can never catch up, learn the code, and be accepted' (p. xv). Certainly, New Criticism, though not chronologically presented in this timeline, continues to enforce a principle of the 'close reading' of students' texts to determine the choices a writer has made, or as Philip Roth contends 'the executed result of the author's intentions' (qtd. in Grimes, 1999: 15). Roth decides that 'when a student enters a Workshop seminar room, any hope of being rescued by the abstractions of theory vanishes the moment discussions begin' (qtd. in Grimes, 1999: 15). He notes that the workshop leaders, having 'jettisoned genius and ignored literary theory' in the interest of 'the nurture and love of literature', have 'reduced' workshops 'to the teaching of craft' (qtd. in Grimes, 1999: 15). And yet these literary conventions of craft as 'formal strategies' are, as William Faulkner said at the University of Virginia in 1957, the ' "tools" in a writer's workshop' (qtd. in Guevara, 1998).

Today, some believe that the workshop has 'shift[ed] in focus from the text as autonomous object to the text as a construction of the reader' (Garber & Ramjerdi, 1994: 10). Centering the reader in a rhetorical axiology (a social conception of writing), creates a whole new set of considerations, that Eugene Garber and Jan Ramjerdi report 'were suppressed in a formalist perspective' (p. 10). With the 'elevation and redefinition of the role of the reader from a neutral observer to an active participant', the workshop is said to take on a more dynamic atmosphere. (Garber & Ramjerdi, 1994: 11). When the text is no longer isolated, 'its boundaries are no longer clearly there'; therefore, 'political and ideological issues ... emerge' (Garber & Ramjerdi, 1994: 11). The argument here is that more is at stake in this workshop setting as there are issues of audience to consider – personal preferences, prejudices and such – or depending on the specifics of the classroom, 'audience' may imply a discourse community which considers not personal priorities, but the expectations that compositionist Patricia Bizzell (1982: 218) informs us, are 'share[d] by the virtue of belonging to that particular community'. More is at stake, Garber and Ramjerdi conclude, because there is no longer an 'object of study that filters, directs, constrains, and distances response' (Garber & Ramjerdi, 1994: 14–15).

This history does not suggest that workshop teachers overtly subscribe to one axiology over another or that there are not overlapping approaches. In fact, in many cases, alternate workshop practices and approaches exist, some of which are discussed below. This historical account does, however, shed some light on workshop approaches and attitudes as influenced by university needs, writers' practices and cultural relativism, not to mention *how* what we do changes with each generation. The past events demonstrate to some extent, the ways in which literary studies has dominated creative writing and how the theory of composition and rhetoric has often informed the theory of creative writing. Vandenberg (2004) rightly includes the training of creative writers as composition teachers in this intersection, and I might add that the number of creative writing teachers who also teach composition as part of their course load has been rising since Moxley (1989: 27) urged educators to 'be careful not to confuse the single cell for the organism', and Wendy Bishop (1994) addressed her writer-teacher/ teacher-writing perspective on blurring the boundaries between composition and creative writing in the early nineties. Although there is much more that is relevant to the history of the writing workshop and, by extension, the field of creative writing, reproaches regarding the workshop's practice-based pedagogy, its bureaucratization, its breed of sameness and questionable theoretical and intellectual value, and its suggested apathetic interest in reform, are pressing concerns that make championing the workshop as the profession's signature pedagogy no small task.

Perceptions and Practice

Our Students

If it were possible to construct our students' profile, we would need to consider the vast diversity of all who enroll in our workshop classes, their values and traditions, their motivations and their preferred method for learning. Not to consider such variables might generate stereotypes and assumptions. Although as educators, we cannot assemble such a character sketch – it is impossible really, outrageous even to envision – we *can*, however, appraise the wide range of sociological and cultural research and studies that issue collective perspectives on forces that bear influence on the students we teach in higher education, factors that impact our students' interest *in* creative writing and their ability to learn and respond to our modes of teaching. As such, teachers *can* assess their students' motivations for signing up for their workshops. They can and should draw on these conclusions and their usefulness as it relates to the (re)construction of their workshop design.

Today, we teach the Google Generation. These 'Tech-savvy "Millennials"', as Scott Carlson (2005) describes them in his *The Chronicle of Higher Education* article entitled 'The Net Generation goes to college', 'have lots of gadgets, like to multitask, and expect to control what, when, and how they learn'. Our students think differently; their attention is scattered, their concentration diffused. We are no longer of the mindset that 'the 100 billion or so neurons inside our skulls are largely fixed by the time we reach adulthood' (Carr, 2008). Our students have begun to take on the qualities of 'our intellectual technologies' – their brains are 'adapting ... at a biological level', says writer Nicholas Carr. In his 2008 *The Atlantic* article 'Is Google making us stupid?', Carr complains that '[i]mmersing myself in a book or a lengthy article used to be easy. My mind would get caught up in the narrative ... and I'd spend hours strolling through long stretches of prose'. No longer is that possible, Carr admits. 'Now my concentration often starts to drift after two or three pages', he notes; 'I get fidgety, lose a thread, begin looking for something else to do'. For Carr, 'the deep reading that used to come naturally has become a struggle'. These 'troubles' are not dissimilar to the experiences of his friends and acquaintances who are, mostly, 'literary types'. Kathryn Tyler (2007), author of 'The tethered generation', specifies that individuals born after 1978 tend to have difficulty thinking for themselves without the tethered advice from parents or significant others who are just a text or speed dial away. They struggle with patience, with detail-oriented tasks such as those required for writing and proofreading, and also with attention to social conventions and understanding what it means to focus and work hard.

A common observation of the Net Generation is its tendency toward self-absorption, a perception that runs parallel to the one which situates our students as self-gratifiers with inflated egos, liberated from oppressed influences and immersed in an American culture of disposability and commodification. The emphasis on feelings, a fundamental absolute of progressive education, persists as a dominant postmodern philosophy in our educational system. As a result, some students come to us with Romantic notions of writing their poems and stories in one long, uninterrupted stream of consciousness. They have ideations of talent – they've been writing their whole lives. Mark Wallace (CA State University, San Marcos), a respondent of my workshop survey, has seen some of these preconceptions play out in his classroom. He notes, 'students often come into my courses with high expectations about their futures as writers and are sometimes shocked to discover how much time and effort it takes to write well'. Additionally, Monica Berlin (Knox College) contends 'students often misunderstand what our job there is'. She observes, 'they often come into workshop expecting we will disregard all notions of graciousness, and in doing so they often do not take the work on its own terms'.

Problems created by lack of experience are sometimes compounded by a lack of motivation and a lack of talent. One instructor admits 'I don't want to spend time workshopping sloppy, incomplete, last minute efforts'. Lorna Jackson (University of Victoria) asserts 'students are still reluctant to commit themselves to a schedule of practice', and Martin Cockroft

(Waynesburg University) adds 'students tend to undervalue the 90% of the time spent reading and talking about OTHER students' poems and stories'. Because of this perception, he contends 'a few students put very little effort into prepping for workshop (e.g. they write few comments, have lost the poems for that day, or have little of substance to say)'. For Gaylene Perry (Deakin University, Melbourne, Australia), lack of effort translates to students 'not reading drafts in time for class or the workshopping student not supplying a draft in time'. She considers this 'to be a new problem for us, perhaps partly due to university pressure to let more students enroll in our program. In the past, she submits, 'the classes were smaller, the skill levels higher, and the commitment and preparedness much greater'.

While I am aware that these comments may generalize students' lack of effort, it is also clear (as some workshop survey responders specify) that a complicated history buttresses students' engagement with their coursework. It is a history that significantly precedes the day students sign up for creative writing courses or the day they enter creative writing classrooms. Concerns of program design and class size, open admission policies and a long well-documented history by the NEA of poor reading skills and comprehension at the college-level coupled with fewer opportunities for the reading of literature in college shadows our students' profile. Although there are many more influences, certainly the focus of this section on the Net Generation and all that it bears is a major contributing agent.

Some suggest that what motivates students to seek out creative writing workshop classes may be because they want 'freedom from an oppressive curriculum that demands too much rote critical thinking, dry textual analysis, and academic prose strangled by thesis statements and Strunk & White correctness' (Healey, 2009: 32). Catherine Cole (2007: 7) agrees, citing a panel of researchers who note that 'society's emphasis on success, instant gratification, the retail/consumer model of education' as well as 'student-centered approaches to learning, lead students to look for easy answers and to count on high grades, to avoid difficult work and to develop inflated perceptions of their abilities'. Edmund Hansen and James Stevens implicate our students' 'low tolerance for challenge', their 'risk averse' posture in our classrooms as products of 'educational consumerism and an institutional focus on assessment' (qtd. in Cole, 2007: 7).

Others sit in our workshop for reasons still valid in Stephen Minot's (1976) assessment of student motives, some which involve therapy and a childish love of language. They may enroll in our workshops, according to Light's (1999: 4) study, for an opportunity to write in a structure that provides 'an interactive writing environment with experts/tutors and peers'. While they may find a place in the circles of desks creative writing teachers construct for community sake, it may be because they assume their workshops will not only be fun and engaging, but also easy. I would second the response of teachers who note how their students are surprised by how much hard work goes into the practice of writing and how vigorous this coursework can be.

These are, in part, our undergraduate writing students – writing majors, business majors, nursing students, marine biologists, those undecided. A few may come unprepared to class; many come with little or no reading experience. How are creative writing educators to connect with students who are preoccupied with a virtual rather than a physical world, students who are more likely to skip university lectures and less likely to go to the library and check out a book? Are our writing students among the average college graduates who have 'spent less than 5,000 hours of their lives reading, but over 10,000 hours playing video games (not to mention 20,000 hours of watching TV)', as Marc Prensky (2001) claims in 'Digital natives, digital immigrants'? We do know that our students are among the majority who want technology at the ready. 'The more portable the better', Carlson (2005) notes. After all, he suggests, 'they are able to juggle a conversation on Instant Messenger, a Web-surfing session, and an iTunes playlist while reading *Twelfth Night* for homework'. Are creative writing teachers ready to embrace and prepare for changes that suit these Googlers – to construct workshops online, create videos and modules, craft lectures on podcasts, which can then be downloaded to students' iPods, becoming portable, rewindable, even pauseable? Should they be?

While this generation may depend on the 'tethering' that Kathryn Tyler (2007) addresses to feel secure in its decision-making, it is also a population which works well in group environments. 'Millennials' are familiar with diversity, more accepting of non-traditional relationships and rhetorical situations. Perhaps the physicality of our small class size attracts students to our workshops. They are a creative bunch; experts at multitasking, at thinking out of the box – and their creativity – the 'buzzword of the business world' – has real market value claims Steve Healey (2009) in his essay 'The rise of creative writing & the new value of creativity'. Healey reports that business recruiters are presently visiting top arts graduate schools looking for candidates for their corporations. This is because, as Daniel H. Pink, author of 'The MFA is the new MBA' published in *Harvard Business Review*, says, 'the basic financial skills learned in the MBA program are quickly becoming obsolete ... The tasks that remain ... increasingly involve creativity' (Pink, qtd. in Healey, 2009: 34). Businesses, looking to distinguish their products and services 'in today's overstocked, materially abundant marketplace', are seeking alternatives, creativity, ways 'to make their offerings transcendent – physically and emotionally compelling' (Pink, qtd. in Healey, 2009: 34).

Creative writing students are deeply immersed in the digital world and are part of a historical moment that Thomas L. Friedman, author of the bestseller *The World is Flat: A Brief History of the Twenty-First Century*, coins 'The New Age of Creativity'. Friedman connects communications technology and the occasion for people interested in 'authoring their own content' (qtd. in Healey, 2009: 34), particularly, Healey adds, 'in easily manipulated digital format' (p. 34). Creative writing students can make this 'leap', Healey accurately suggests, 'from the new authors of the digital networks to the new authors of the Creative Writing workshops' (p. 35) with better pedagogical planning in our workshop-based classrooms. Robert Coover cautions that if literary artists do *not* 'gravitate toward this powerful medium [electronic/digital modalities] ... if literature does not in fact find a place there, then the vast majority of the human race will simply do without it, and thus, whether the new generations know it or not, they (all of us) will be greatly impoverished' (qtd. in Bruns & Brien, n.d.).

Much has been written about the holistic purpose of creative writing and the writing workshop and its noble ability to make our students more rounded citizens. These are echoes of the egalitarian principles of Deweyan education, which advance the democratization of creative power (reiterations of Emerson). Healey cites the Romantic mission statement of AWP, Jane Ciabattari's (2005) *Poets & Writers* essay 'Workshop: A revolution of sensibility', and D.W. Fenza's (2000) defense of creative writing in the academy in 'Creative writing & its discontents' as proselytizing these views. AWP adopts the artist as 'outsider, set apart from the standardized triteness of institutions' (Healey, 2009: 32); Ciabattari (2005) refers to the 'willed discipline through which students learn to shape and order their perceptions of an ever more complicated world around them'; and Fenza (2000) strengthens creative writing's otherness when he says:

> [L]ike other lessons of creative writing – creativity, empathy, persuasiveness, expression, and aesthetic discernment – the artistic experience of the will's efficacy may seem too rarefied a goal for a practical age that prefers to quantify success in patents, cures, sales units, and dollars.

Healey thinks not, and I agree with him. While poems and stories are valued products of the workshop, there is more to be learned through the model's process, more 'front loading' as Henley calls it, pedagogy 'with interventions in the writing process before it begins and while it's happening, instead of the more traditional back-loading – that is, intervening after a written product already exists' (p. 38).

Creative writing teachers miss opportunities to design more vigor in their writing workshops, when they lag behind as a field, Healey suggests, a field which also falters in the 'development of a reflexive theoretical framework that would make it more aware of its real social value and its real social effects, and this lag has encouraged further lag in revisions of its teaching methods' (p. 38). Creative writing students may be ahead of educators in the discipline in terms of 'thinking out of the box' if teachers consider that as part of an institutionalized field, they generally continue to think of themselves as still 'inside the box'.

Our Critics

As creative writing teachers we may be insulated by our marginalized (sometimes self-imposed) home within English departments, but we are not cocooned to complaints about the model's effectiveness by critics who do not sit in our workshop circles or at our tables of writers. Complaints about the lack of intelligence in the workshop design come by way of faculty tensions or exclusions from department decisions or overt or obscure charges in journal articles and/or editorials, and possibly at professional conference sessions. Creative writers are not necessarily compliant with the department's mission or held to the same scholarly standards that dominate the profession as a whole. In fact, creative writers often make further distinctions between the department profession and *their* profession. Many believe that their poems and stories, also known as their 'hallmarks for success', which may be published in respectable but not always nationally-recognized journals and presses, are treated like flimsy, onion-skinned tissue paper. Their conferences are sometimes tabled as artsy. Even their professional organization fails to re-envision their discipline, its teachers, its mode of instruction – *its workshop*.

This kind of criticism and divide has a long history despite the continued contribution that creative writing programs bring to the English department. My intent in laying out these interdepartmental issues is not meant to aggravate what Ben Siegel (1989: 7) refers to as 'bruised sensitivities' between creative writing and literary studies; derisions which in the past 'appeared most bitter and open'. On the contrary, I suggest that *creative writing studies* can stand alongside literary studies and composition studies with its value-added scholarship, its renewed workshop pedagogy (complete with markers of professional difference) and hybrid models that include more specialized course offerings and more creative arts focus that better prepares our students for creative industries.

Our Teachers

Creative writing teachers make efforts to monitor the pulse of the workshop as Karl Elder (Lakeland College) does, gauging the needs of his students by offering 'models of strong work that will appeal to their unique sensibilities'. Likewise, my workshop survey indicates that creative writing teachers try to engage with students as individuals rather than abstractions. One instructor 'finds their issues and challenges' and in this pursuit, s/he discovers 'who they are, their passions and goes from there'. Similarly, Robert Boswell (New Mexico State University) considers the individuality of his students by affirming 'that every student is taught in every class, not just the student whose story is being discussed'. To personalize his workshop course, Keith Kumasen Abbott (Naropa) makes adjustments based on student responses to his first week survey, while Jane Hilberry (Colorado College) dismantles her workshop by teaching 'on a model of improvisation, each course and each class different, depending on what the students bring to the course'.

Some creative writing teachers *are* responding to the 'shifting nature of students' readings in new media, film, and digitized images, music/texts' (Cole, 2007: 7) by adding digital writing workshops. The University of Massachusetts Amherst, for example, transitions students to write in the new digital age by offering courses like 'Telling it Straight, Telling it Slant, Telling it Digital'. George Mason University offers an introduction to digital writing in the genres as part of its creative writing concentration program. Janet McCann (Texas A & M) has a 'section on hypertext poetry and using computers in poetry', and Valerie Martinez (College at Santa Fe) includes in her course, 'a study of cyberpoetics'. Judith Baumel (Adelphi University) uses 'wikis, blogs, and Moodle to teach the workshops', and one teacher 'encourages the use of graphics and the material nature of what they are making' when they construct and 'distribute their own books'. Many universities across the globe include creative writing media as part of their undergraduate creative writing courses. What else is possible in the creative writing workshop-based classroom? How might we engage students as content creators for digital media and become more familiar with hypertext media theory and practice? In what ways might creative writing programs merge with other programs or other program concepts and bring these ideas/designs into our workshops?

Our Workshop Pedagogy

In the workshop chronicle above, I address ways in which creative writing's history confines and complicates its practice. The structure of creative writing in terms of its praxes and principles and the structure of the workshop – to the degree that this method of instruction is, for many teachers, the primary pedagogy of creative writing – finds itself divaricated. Just what are creative writing teachers doing in the workshop model? Some workshop teachers advance the Romantic perceptions of student writers. Ostrom contends we might locate 'some of the [current] resistance to conceptualizing teaching back to resilient Romantic theory (Blake, Wordsworth, Coleridge, Keats, Emerson, Whitman, Ginsberg)' where '[p]edagogy and theory become incidental at best in the egotistically sublime pedagogy of the self' (Ostrom, 1994: xv). Here, situated in Romantic terms, the writer 'has no particular use for teachers or workshops; "he" was born with author-ity, with authorizing talent, with genius, with a potency, with a "repetition in the finite mind" (as Coleridge would have it) "of the infinite I Am"' (p. xv). Given this Romantic belief, '[h]e is godlike – Dionysian, Promethean, mercurial. He is gifted and blessed; he's got what it takes' (p. xv). The workshop teacher who advances these notions or who is unaware of their pitfalls faces challenges in the workshop dealing with authority and revision practices.

Maurice Kilwein Guevara (1998) questions teaching practices rooted in such Romantic notions of the imagination as 'sacred' and 'intangible' and 'to tamper with it is taboo'. He laments workshop practices that do little to exercise what we as teachers desire to promote in our students: 'originality, imagination, and creativity'. Other instructors may be guided by the sensibilities of humanistic practices of the cultural and intellectual call for a renewal of academy and culture initiated by Irving Babbitt and Norman Foerster. The humanistic workshop teacher promotes the early academic goals of writing for its own sake, for the overall improvement of students' writing inside and outside academia. These workshop-based classrooms are less interested in more complicated programmatic goals that might help establish writers for teaching, publication or other possible creative career development.

Most often critiqued is the workshop practice that promotes expressivist practices that are based on principles of self-expression and inspiration. Other workshop models include feminist pedagogies, which tend to decenter models of inspiration and traditional master-apprentice type workshop models. Feminist pedagogy influences such teachers as Mary Ann Cain, Nancy Welch and Katherine Haake – craft critics who promote less formal structures and more of what Haake (2005: 98) refers to as the 'dismantling [of] authority'. Reader-response theories in the workshop model are likely the least practiced approach, while New Criticism in its close reading practices of professional stories and student texts is a workshop praxis which informs the ways many of us come to understand and interpret exemplary texts and student manuscripts.

As addressed earlier, presenting students with a multi-faceted approach to reading and writing offers writers more writing options and practice. Bizzaro (1993: xv) considers how these variable methods mirror 'the range of possible relationships between student and teacher'. As such, we might become more aware of the authority dynamics in the classroom, the dialectical relationships that exist in our workshops. Gayle Elliott (1994: 114) asks us *not* to see our role in the workshop as 'the teacher-of-the-students and the students-of-the-teacher', but rather as '*teacher-student with students-teachers* ... a communal model' where 'the students generate the "texts" for the course', and 'engender the tenor and scope of the criticism' (author's italics). Peter Elbow promotes a more equitable status in the classroom, 'encourag[ing] instructors to surrender the trappings of traditional teacherly authority', so that they might 'act as a member of the class' "writing community"' instead (qtd. in Kuhl, 2005: 11).

Finally, composition's rhetorical strategies bear a strong influence on our workshop model. Early scholarship presents the ways in which composition and creative writing might share writing strategies beginning with Joseph Moxley (1989), forged ahead by Wendy Bishop (1994) and later, as supported by Tim Mayers and most recently by Douglas Hesse (2011) and Dianne Donnelly (2011). As a teacher of creative writing and composition studies, I admit to the ways in which composition's rhetorical practices have influenced my workshop dynamics and how creative writing techniques have added depth to first-year composing and persuasion. Writing teachers who are also composition instructors and those who engage in creative writing scholarship through publications and/or conferences often talk about how writing out long passages of criticism helps to strengthen their creative works and how description and imagery, for example, in stories and poems, aids in adding more depth to scholarship. I welcome these intersecting influences for the discipline of *creative writing studies*.

What the workshop model needs now is a rigorous inquiry into its practices, a more thorough understanding of how its history impacts our pedagogies, a study on what motivates our students, how they learn and how we might open the workshop space to other alternatives – to more program designs. We are prime, not for annexation, as Vandenberg suggests, but for more independence through the development of *creative writing studies*.

Flexing the Workshop Shape or Opening the Space to Alternatives

The success of the writing workshop along with our students' corresponding success in the workshop model is relative in terms of standards of measurement. In some cases, student publication is still the primary institutional aim as there is pressure to produce results to sustain program visibility and enrollment, even at the undergraduate level. This more global objective may be contrary for the teacher who uses the workshop as a platform for students to acquire and practice fundamentals, for more risk-taking activities and experimentation, and for opportunities to emphasize process and explore *how* a story or poem unfolds.

On the other hand, department goals may disclaim a teacher's expertise and privilege a workshop space in which student feedback carries more weight than a teacher's technical knowledge. In many institutions, program design is in the hands of administration and guided by bottom line costs and profit margins. The success of the workshop is largely contingent on class size, particularly at the introductory level. Ideally, a workshop class could be well-managed with 10 students. Martin Cockroft (Waynesburg University) has 17 students in his introductory class; some have 25 or more – and, with the advent of university cut-backs in a stressed economy that limits or excludes the hiring of new faculty, class sizes are increasing, exponentially. Given the increased class size, Karen Holmberg (Oregon State) attests, 'if we were to workshop all poems in the class, we would only have time to write 3 poems a term'. Lorna Jackson (University of Victoria) admits that 'as a fiction teacher, at certain times of the semester' she is 'unable to read the volume of work in a reasonable work week'. Furthermore, oversize classes can lead to students spending excessive amounts of time 'reading the works of student writers rather than those of more accomplished writers' (Deanna Kern Ludwin, Colorado State). Course workload and the mix of majors and non-majors in workshop courses are other issues for teachers like Lex Runciman (Linfield College), who notes, 'we struggle to meet student demand, and recent assessment feedback from our creative writing majors tells us they wish we had more "majors only" courses'.

Some suggest entry requirements for enrolling in a creative writing class, particularly an upper level class, would lead to more authentic learning opportunities and more serious student commitment. There are more colleges and institutions that offer creative writing classes without a major or minor than there are BFA or minor tracts or associate degree programs. Wendy Bishop and David Starkey (2006: 198) suggest the 'workshop has led to an unprecedented democratization of imaginative writing in America'.

In fact, they conclude, 'now that nearly every American high school and community college offers at least one creative writing class, access to basic instruction in the art is widely available' (p. 198). Given the recent expanse of the field that Ritter and Vanderslice (2007: xviii) address in their introduction to *Can It Really Be Taught?: Resisting Lore in Creative Writing Pedagogy*, such a proliferation of program development should give us pause to rethink creative writing's pedagogy to include the workshop model by 'reassessing specific patterns and practices'. Such rapid program development might also serve to further dilute the significance of a creative writing degree. Imagine, some teachers ask, that anyone can declare himself or herself a creative writing major or that anyone can take a creative writing course with little or no experience. The experience of such indiscrimination, according to one unnamed instructor, leads to a class 'filled with a lot of disinterested, unengaged, untalented students'. Not just untalented, s/he notes, but 'students who actually have significant writing problems; students who need to retake composition, even'.

In fact, the survey suggests that many students can take creative writing to satisfy an elective, and/or to satisfy a creative writing program requirement and/or a writing intensive requirement. To this claim, Juliet Davis (University of Tampa) responds, 'this should not be the case'. She grants that 'one of our biggest challenges is the fact that students can take creative writing to satisfy both a writing intensive requirement and a humanities requirement'. For 60% of the programs surveyed, students are not required to take a prerequisite to an introductory creative writing course.

There are many influences that complicate the workshop space that range from the teacher's appropriation of student work and/or the presumption of style to the more global call for us to attend to the poor reading and comprehension skills of our students as reported in the latest NEA report. We are now being asked to 'focus our attention and resources on an activity both fundamental and irreplaceable for democracy' (Gioia, qtd. in Burriesci, 2008: 2). My point in emphasizing factors that bear influence on the workshop model is twofold: first, as Stephen Minot (1976: 35) long ago suggests, teachers should 'draw on a full range of tastes and address particular student motives for coming to the creative writing classroom', and second, teachers must reconsider their program design, addressing what one teacher in my survey calls 'one of the narrowest educations ... especially if most of its courses are run with the traditional workshop model'.

Students' motives girdle my second point which begins with the advancement of two possible workshop trajectories at the undergraduate level. The first path functions as a series of courses under the general education track for the appreciation of literature through writing and one that centers on a degree program situated for the advancement of writing (and reading) for its own sake (creative writing's early pedagogical goal). Coursework at the general education level might include 'The Craft of Fiction' (or poetry or drama), 'Writing Processes', 'Reading as a Writer', 'Form and Technique', 'Narration and Description'; perhaps, genre writing, digital options, creative essays, nature and travel writing, writing the environment and literary hypertext. A course that addresses the lore of creative writing would be illuminating. Considering some of the courses noted above, I see the workshop setting for this track in any number of ways: as a pairing of partners, a small network, a larger writing community and/or a one-on-one student-teacher conference. The workshop would provide a place for students to experiment, take risks, develop skills, share work and advance creative and critical thinking.

This program track might also incorporate more panoramic goals to include, among others, an outward attention to public spheres. I see this offering as one open to all undergraduates; perhaps, even as a course option that is required of first-year students for the purpose of satisfying 'rigorous standards' (Clark, 1999) set by English departments. This option considers the popularity and growth of creative writing and the workshop model while understanding that the goals of this path are noble in their encompassing nature.

The second baccalaureate program track considers the intermediate and advanced creative writer, one whose placement in the program is dependent on a sample of student work. While not excluding some of the coursework outlined above, the curriculum for this track should be more robust and inclusive. At this level students should understand and apply variable critical approaches to reading and writing. With a secondary goal toward flexing the elasticity of the workshop, students might be exposed to other performative arts in an effort to broaden their expanse of writing. This interdisciplinary approach introduces more outlets for expression, more venues for creativity, more activity and demonstration and more synthesis, analysis, process, production. This might mean a sharing of workshops between the arts; perhaps, a dialogue that is acted by drama students, action that is produced on stage and/or poems expressed in music, painting, sculpture, dance. Ostrom (1994), in his introduction to *Colors of a Different Horse*, wonders how creative writing might be linked to 'the street'. He asks, 'Who among us is already inviting rap, hip-hop, performance poetry and other so-called popular sources of compositional improvisation into our workshop?' (p. xxii). Although not all instructors agree with the kind of performative art that Ostrom addresses, nor are all teachers interested in employing technological techniques in their classrooms, there exist many creative writing teachers who *have* initiated some movement in other creative arts disciplines. For example, Gaylene Perry (Deakin University) speaks of 'dance studio sessions or visual arts life drawing classes', where students can 'practice' their work. Donald Platt (Purdue) has partnered with a visual arts class, 'visiting their studio for 1–2 class sessions and writing poems from their work. In turn', he says, 'we gave them poems that were not inspired by art, and the artists used them to generate drawings and paintings'.

Similarly, Lisa Russ Spaar (University of Virginia) team-teaches 'a poetry/printmaking workshop in which students collaborate (the printmakers write poems, the poets print, and they work together to produce low and high-end books'. Mekeel McBride (University of New Hampshire) asks students 'to invent or make a musical instrument, then write a poem and accompany the poem with the instrument'. She notes, 'people have used Volvo car engines, crystal glasses filled with water, etc'. McBride claims this exercise 'teaches [creative writers] to listen to sound in a whole different way'. In Martin Cockroft's (Waynesburg University) workshop class, students listen to recordings of poets reading. He has shown them 'YouTube videos of slam poets and animated poems (e.g. Billy Collins and others)'. Cockroft also introduces his class to useful websites such as *'Poetry Daily*, the *Penn Sounds* poetry archive, online journals, and writers' blogs'. Another teacher plans to establish a web page that she will 'seed' with an opening sentence. She'll permit students 'to add or delete anything at any time and see what we have at semester's end'. At the 2010 Conference on College Composition and Communication (CCCC), one writer addressed the teaching of fiction as a method for creating games. Students as producers of games (Gamebrix, Scratch, Stagecast) advance the concept of game learning (much like online learning). James Paul Gee (2003), author of *What Video Games Have to Teach Us About Learning and Literacy*, considers the 'Gaming Generation' (part of the Net Generation), which is said to learn differently than previous generations. He suggests that students of the gaming generation become insiders, teachers, and producers when they create environments, interactive stories, characters and animation.

Film clips are used by Deanna Kern Ludwin (Colorado State) to 'illustrate dialogue and the use of metaphor'. She adds, '*Il Postino* is great for this'. At the three-year MFA program at the University of North Carolina at Wilmington, Philip Gerard notes that students 'write dialogue, and then see it performed by actors in a black-box theater on campus ... They watch films to learn how to build scenes better' (Delaney, 2007). Keith Kumasen

Abbott (Naropa) also uses media – 'drama and documentary – usually in the opening 8 weeks – but very sparingly in terms of length'. He never uses an entire film during a workshop, and will also introduce 'artists and musicians and their art or music to discuss organizational principles'. Film can be used to demonstrate dialogue techniques – dramatic and comedic clips in films such as *Before the Sunset* to show how dialogue delves into relationship issues, or a snippet of *Princess Bride* as an example of a dialogue that takes a serious situation and deals with it in a comedic fashion, or a preview of *Doubt* to accentuate how dialogue can convey conflict, urgency, power. The film clips can be followed with discussion and writing – prompts that allow students to practice writing in new ways. Film as a venue can also illuminate scene development and the credibility of details, setting and atmosphere.

This program course might include more interdisciplinary activity – perhaps a literary studies course that embraces creative projects or a theory course that experiments with the construction of writing. Creative attention to workshop development should also include student and group research and presentations. At this level, working collaboratively in small groups, creative writing students are empowered to choose stories, facilitate discussions and design exercises to demonstrate and practice processes in such a way that is different than what students do in literature and composition. We might intersect with ways in which social and cultural hierarchies and contrasting ideologies impact our roles as writer and reader. Deweyan principles of 'doing' are advanced here, not to mention a shifting of master-apprentice assumptions. Moreover, these are the type of activities which Haake refers to as linking with the world, and Argie Manolis (2005: 49) refers to as 'outside of academia', the engagement that occurs beyond the classroom defined as 'teacher, writers whose work is studied, peers, and student author'. Deanna Kern Ludwin (Colorado State), for example, takes her class on field trips such as 'campus art galleries to stimulate writing'. This concept is not unfamiliar to Julie Carr (University of Colorado Boulder) whose class writes 'on location together'. Carr suggests that in her class, 'It's never just "write a poem." There are always things to try'. Additionally, a workshop course that includes what our students might do with a creative writing degree would be well-attended – one that offers multiple perspectives, visiting lecturers – real practical exposure. In both baccalaureate tracks we should not forget 'that our aim should be to foster more dedicated writers' (Royster, 2005: 27), a goal Royster claims we often lose as we engage in other pursuits.

Our universities and colleges might pilot more courses and programs that engage critically and creatively with a range of artistic disciplines to afford a direction that goes beyond the realms of traditional creative writing courses and text production. *Creative writing studies* might take the lead in such development, offering many different areas of creative practices that best reflect the burgeoning creative economy opportunities that exist for creative writers in film, journalism, digital communication, television, design drama, new media and more. We might look to programs underway that have responded to industry demand for graduates with expertise in several creative areas. For example, in the United Kingdom, Bangor University's The School of Creative Studies and Media offers Bachelor of Arts study that combines theoretical and critical approaches with hands-on creative practices to include Professional Writing and Journalism, Media and Digital Communication, Film Studies, Performance Studies and Creative and Media Practice.[4] Understanding that 'interdisciplinarity is integral to the life of a creative professional',[5] The Bachelor of Creative Industries degree at Queensland University of Technology (Australia), offers majors in the following: Animation; Art and Design History; Creative and Professional Writing; Dance Studies; Digital Media; Drama; Entertainment Industries; Fashion; Film, Television and Screen; Interactive and Visual Design; Journalism, Media and Communication; Literary Studies; Music. Such 'popularity of the concept of creativity' goes 'far beyond the discipline of creative writing and the creative arts', Perry (2010: 128) tells us and what this means for the dynamic workshop model is that it 'will continue to morph and merge, indeed continuing to turn up in academic disciplines not traditionally likely to use such a model in their teaching'.

In addition to such development in creative industries, a carefully coordinated program that includes a series of mini-lectures on relevant topics might interest a large number of students, could defray costs and might be managed over shorter six to eight week semesters. Workshop breakout sessions might follow these lectures to advance writing and discussion relevant to lecture topics. With such variability, rigor and relativity, there would be no need to dismantle the workshop for undergraduate students.

At the MFA level, the same course direction might exist, with pedagogical differences. For example, splitting the MFA track into two paths opens possibilities for the writer who is interested in advancing her writing. The other track might include writers who are also interested in the pedagogy of creative writing, *creative writing studies*, composition; the interdisciplinary approach to teaching creative composing practices, the reciprocal relationship between creative practice, theory and research. A complementary or overlapping track might include a concentration on creativity in the marketplace. Think of the exciting coursework, internships and relevancy to such a program design with conscious departures from traditional models. Right now, creative writing certificates and concentrations are provided in some universities for the business major. Why not apply this practice as part of the MFA career track, perhaps inviting corporate recruiters to classes as well as creative writing faculty team teaching with business and communications faculty? Craft critics Mayers and Starkey, in particular, also advocate for the splitting of the MFA into two directions. Finally, the workshop at the PhD level might be more variable than the tired 'shopping' of 'works' to include more critical exigency, teacher training and relative coursework that considers Bizzaro's (2004: 301) suggestions of coursework such as 'Research in Creative Writing', 'Pedagogy of Creative Writing' and 'Professional Issues in Creative Writing' as a means of 'connect[ing] research skills typically stressed in English departments with skills stressed in creative-writing instruction'.

Rather than pitching a one-stop workshop or pitting creativity against criticism or constructing a crustacean shell as Haake (2007: 16) admits to doing at one time around her practice, 'stubbornly insist[ing] that we commit ourselves ... to an examination of what happens in the writing moment to let writing take place', we might get more creative and purposeful with our workshop design to better serve our students, our teachers and our field.

Our Lore

Perceptions of creative writing are perpetuated by its lore – a topic, which binds the essays in Ritter and Vanderslice's (2007) collection *Can It Really Be Taught?: Resisting Lore in Creative Writing Pedagogy*. Lore is defined by Stephen North as 'the accumulated body of traditions, practices, and beliefs ... that influence how writing is done, learned and taught' (qtd. in Ritter & Vanderslice, 2007: xiii). Moreover, North ascribes 'anything' to the component of lore, insisting that '[o]nce somebody says [something] has worked or is working or might work, it is part of lore' (qtd. in Ritter & Vanderslice, 2005: 107). His more disquieting feature concerns our discussion about the questionable effectiveness of the workshop, in that 'while anything can become a part of lore, nothing can be dropped from it either. There is simply no mechanism for it' (qtd. in Ritter & Vanderslice, 2005: 107–108).

Consequently, the century-old workshop model, a pedagogy which has been perhaps marginally revised and sustained as lore, has governed the workshop-based creative writing classroom, regardless of its usefulness or application. In fact, my survey results as well as Delaney's (2007) report, note the range of variability of the workshop's appliance. Delaney cites that, depending on whom one is asking, 'workshops are always useful, sometimes useful, or never useful'. Regardless of the verdict, the workshop is critically a part of creative writing's lore and as such, North informs, cannot be withdrawn or altered. While North claims we can 'argue for the value' of what others 'hold in ... low esteem' (qtd. in Ritter & Vanderslice, 2005: 108), this 'stand requires that practitioners first reflect on, examine, and challenge their own institutionally inherited practices in the interest of rendering them more robust' (Ritter & Vanderslice, 2005: 108). While we may attempt to challenge such practices, to vivify and render them more robust, it is nonetheless difficult to intercept and reverse the lore of the workshop model and the commodification of popular images of writing and writers, which draw some of our students to our workshops.

Such lore manifests in popular magazines and inspirational guides such as *The Artist's Way*, *The Vein of Gold* and *Simple Abundance* or commercial handbooks that infer anyone can be a writer. For example, in a collection from *The Washington Post Book World*, popular novelist Mary Higgins Clark (2003), in an essay titled 'Touched by an angel', addresses a question often asked in interviews as to when she decided to become a writer. Her response perpetuates the lore that writing cannot be taught but rather that talent is innate, blessed, in fact, by one's fabled patroness. Clark claims, 'I firmly believe that mythical godmothers make appearances at our cradles, and bestow their gifts' (p. 35). One envisions Clark's godmother, wand in hand, standing at her cradle bestowing such a gift, whispering, 'You will be a storyteller' (p. 35). Other authors suggest young writers might learn to write if only they listen to their muse. This same message is conveyed in films like *The Muse*, which depicts a screenwriter's use of a real-life muse to inspire creativity.

Other movies sustain the lore of the writer in ways that romanticize his/her lonely, troubled life in the garret (*Finding Forrester, As Good as it Gets, Big Bad Love, Bullets on Broadway*) or movies that display some manner of a once prolific teacher who suffers writer's block and who is either infused or tortured by the genius of his/her student (*Alex & Emma, Barton Fink, Deathtrap, Deconstructing Harry, Starting Out in the Evening, Wonder Boys*) or films that portray the deranged writer fan (*Misery*) or the alcoholic writer (*Barfly*). Francine Prose's novel *Blue Angel* continues the tale of the middle-aged, creative writing professor who has writer's block. The writer-teacher enjoys trysts with his talented female student who, coincidently, writes, flaunts even, her life-as-art musings in his workshop. In the end, the student gets a book deal and the writer-teacher is told by his editor to give up fiction and pen a memoir about substance abuse. Moreover, popular images of the writer that count Carrie from *Sex and the City* and the industry of self-help writing books including Oprah's role in advocating writing as self-discovery, are the subject of Nancy Kuhl's (2005) essay 'Personal therapeutic writing vs. literary writing'. When students are 'so heavily invested in the popular mythologies dealing with writing and creativity', Kuhl notes, she finds it challenging to make 'meaningful' connections with her students. As long as popular imaging continues to mystify and/or stereotype the writing and writing process, 'instructors of creative writing workshops will increasingly face challenges to their authority' (p. 61). When students are influenced by the lore of creative writing and the expected ease of the writing process, Kuhl notes there is little 'value of any writing process that incorporates criticism, revision, and audience expectations' (p. 61).

Lore is also visible in website advertisements for creative writing programs,[6] even for the notable top-ranked 'rigorous' programs. For example, to study creative writing at Columbia University's School of Art means to 'explore the deep artistic power of language'; at Florida State University, one can enjoy its 'Southern charm, where the roads are lined with live oaks and the world's best oysters are shucked fresh from the Gulf'. At New York University, students attend workshops and 'gather informally, seeking out quiet corners in which to read and write'; the website for Michener Center for Writers notes its location on 'a rolling landscape of limestone bluffs, springs, rivers, and lakes'. Decidedly, the heart of the program at Chatham University lies in its nature, environmental and travel writing. Students travel to such places as Costa Rica, New Zealand, Greece, India and 'generate creative work about the experience'. They offer 'rich opportunities for reflection and meditation'. At Iowa, teachers 'work in large offices where their classes and workshops also meet, like one-room schoolhouses' (Delaney, 2007). Students, like those in Christopher Tilghman's class in Virginia, 'meet in their teachers' living rooms' (qtd. in Delaney, 2007). The advertisements cater to the artistic centering, the quiet serene settings and the atmospheres which might inspire beauty, creativity and inspiration rather than rigor and hard work. Delaney, in a 2007 *Atlantic Monthly* article titled 'Where great writers are made', reports his assessment of America's top graduate writing programs – noting these are the places where students who 'are infected with the fever of the emerging artist' attend. Many students, he says, are 'driven by the implied example of other notable writers who have emerged from one or another program'. The lore, Delaney suggests, is that '[a] single faculty-member writer who's having a notable success often seems to trump a legion of others quietly publishing work that is respected but not widely celebrated'.

Program design often plays into the lore of the easy workshop-based creative writing course. Leahy (2007: 55) bemoans the perception of students who think her class will be an easy 'A', and Michael Cunningham bolsters this mythos when he says that at Brooklyn College, 'unless you simply don't give a shit, you'll get an A' (qtd. in Delaney, 2007). This anti-critical acumen is repeated elsewhere. In the main, Delaney reports, 'professors and program directors characterize their programs as places where writers can find some sanctuary from judgment', or as Columbia's Ben Marcus suggests, at least a setting 'without a lot of hostility to work around' (qtd. in Delaney, 2007). New York University's program director, Chuck Wachtel, sees it less as 'teaching students' as much as 'helping them learn' (qtd. in Delaney, 2007). This sense of helping is forwarded by James Alan McPherson (Iowa's eminence gris) who 'likens [the workshop] to the Midwestern concept of "neighboring", of one crossing the road to help another with a crop' (qtd. in Delaney, 2007). These non-threatening 'neighboring' methods of instruction support the lore that the workshop is an easy conversation, a 'talk fest', one that lacks structure – such risks that James Wilkinson warns us are consequences of our open discussion formats (qtd. in Leahy, 2005: 20).

Adding to this lore is creative writing's absence from the history as a contributor to the ascendancy of English studies. Such invisibility diminishes the concreteness of our discipline, advancing us instead as mysterious, veiled tenants of the English departments that house us. Creative writing is also excluded from the list of addresses for English in the *PMLA Directory*. Lim (2003: 153) reports that while such programs as American Sign Language, Eurasian studies, classics and archaeology, ethic studies and women studies, among others, are listed in the directory, the program listing for creative writing is missing. Conversely, creative writing job postings *are* included in the MLA *Job Information List*. Lim justly concludes that 'by a strange contradiction, creative writing functions visibly as a significant part of the employed profession but remains invisible as part of the discipline' (p. 153).

David Madden signals instructors' culpability in perpetuating lore when he claims he is 'distressed to hear many teachers of writing cater to the romantic preconception of the public and of students when they deny that writing (a mysterious process) can be taught, then go on to claim to achieve far more impossible goals – such as changing a student's life' (qtd. in Ritter & Vanderslice, 2007: xvi). It is no wonder then that teachers like Susan Carol Hauser (Bemidji State) observe that our 'students start writing because they are called to it or driven to it', and 'they stay because they come to understand and love it'. The first may be perpetuated by the lore of becoming a writer, the latter, we hope, is secondary to a rigorous workshop environment that emphasizes the process of writing and the rewards of its practice.

Perhaps more urgent than the lore that impacts our students and program or the critics' complaints, are the voices we find familiar. Perhaps they belong to our creative writing colleagues or, conceivably, we hear our own sentiments echoed in a recent article, on a listserv, at a conference session or in our thoughts as we sit before/among our expecting students, their works-in-progress in hand: the voice asks for something more from the workshop – something else – something better than as one responder to my survey suggests, 'they come to us – this is the best we can do'.

Developing Markers of Professional Difference

Most creative writing teachers are decidedly tepid on the workshop as a traditional pedagogical tool. Yet as Bizzaro (2004: 296) concludes, the model continues because of its tradition rather than any inquiry or study which has proved its effectiveness. This is the lore of the workshop model, the reason why Guevara (1998) says so 'many creative writing workshops seem to drag on like a sled being pulled through a bog of wet snow by a team of faithful dogs' – I suggest that creative writing teachers may be those faithful sledge dogs, and unless they want to continue their 'mushing', they should actively discover their professional markers and ways in which their model can improve. If creative writers are to transform their discipline then they will want to rethink their workshop components, inquire as to the model's effectiveness, revise segments that constitute its rigor and purpose, define how the ways they teach their students to read, write, respond and revise are different than those functions in literary studies and composition studies. Finally, the workshop practice must embrace new theories, teach in new spaces, shift and expand our approaches and view creative writing as a process of discovering new meanings of knowledge.

The Case for Reading and its Distinguishing Markers

The 2008 NEA Report 'To read or not to read' results are even more dismal than the 2004 study, which depict Americans as reading fiction, poetry and drama at a significant lower rate than they were 10 or 20 years earlier. Our college students continue to perform poorly in the 2008 report, with 65% reading for pleasure less than an hour per week or not at all. Students readily argue against this charge, claiming there is little time for reading given the competitive nature of the school system. A corollary item reported in the NEA summary concerns students' distraction by technology. The results suggest 'new media are displacing the intellectual engagement of reading with mere entertainment' (Burriesci, 2008: 2). There is nothing new in this notation since students candidly admit their attentions are limited, and they have trouble narrowing their focus. They know how to twitter, wiki and blog – engage in virtual social activities on Facebook, show emotions using symbols in text, record videos on their cell phones or flip cameras, have YouTube bookmarked on their computers and know all the sources from which to download movies and songs on their laptops, on their iPods and on their Apple iPhones. If they read, they are likely to do so on their iPads or Kindles. They do all of their research on the internet, and while teachers would like to think they are using the library's virtual database, Googlers prefer to – *Google*. They cannot discern the credibility of their sources, and their circuitous route to unsubstantiated knowledge takes them further and further through a deeply-potholed maze of opinions and nuances, so that the credibility of their sources is severely limited. The recently retired NEA Chairman Dana Gioia anticipates a defense for those who might conclude online reading has replaced the hard/softcopy book, when he says the NEA summary 'is not an elegy for the bygone days of print culture, but instead a call to action ... it has enormous consequences for literature and the other arts' (qtd. in Burriesci, 2008: 1).

Some of this lack of reading readiness for our workshop model can be attributed to a culture which seems to have, as one creative writing teacher reports, respect 'for just about anything other than literary culture'. Given the new performative modes of literature, John Meredith Hill (University of Scranton) longs for the tactile pleasure of a book in one's hands, noting that these performative modes 'engage some of our students, in ways that curling up with a thin volume in a corner of the student union while smoking a French or English cigarette (or something) and wearing an intense look was popular among 60s/70s student poets'.

Couple the NEA findings with the manner in which students *read* 'texts' in literary studies classes today, and it becomes clear that our students do not bring the necessary reading acumen to the workshop's round-table discussion. This critical approach to the study of literature proved problematic for novelist Francine Prose (2006) when her passion for reading prompted her interest in graduate school. Here, she thought she would continue her reading of literature; however, her experience served as a warning for what was to come in the decade or so after she dropped out of the program. 'That was when', she says, 'literary academia split into warring camps of deconstructionists, Marxists, feminists, and so forth, all battling for the right to tell students that they were reading "texts" in which ideas and politics trumped what the writer actually wrote' (p. 8). Perhaps, because we experience writing as performance, our fluid form resists such shaping. Sue Roe (2010: 196) suggests that 'because we know that an imaginative piece of writing might be informed as richly by painting, music, dance or theatre as by an in-depth knowledge of literature we have always been reluctant to hook the study of creative writing in a rigid or inflexible way to the study of English literature'.

Gary Hawkins (Warren Wilson College) speaks for many of the creative writing teachers surveyed who contend the workshop model 'works best when students are also enrolled in an array of literature (reading) courses, so that they get a sense of the literary traditions from which they've sprung, and from which they may want to eventually depart'. Although Hawkins specifies that these should be reading courses, the fact remains that literature courses today focus less on the reading of novels and poems and more on what Maurice Manning (Indiana University, Bloomington) refers to as 'literary theory and pseudo-political tracts', which he notes results in work that is 'often boring, self-evident, and poorly written'. The unfortunate realization, Manning observes, is 'when students come to our workshop, we know what they've missed: a basic understanding of the history and tradition of English-language literature'. Leslie Adrienne Miller (University of St Thomas) concurs when she says 'as the discipline of English has moved away from New Critical methods and close reading, it has become more difficult to teach workshops because students do not come into the course with basic analytical skills – which renders the workshop method fairly ineffectual'. Miller finds that more of her time is spent teaching what used to be taught in general literature courses, which she decides considerably interferes with the time she would dedicate to workshopping.

The workshop model which is predicated on critical reading acumen and response skills, often thrusts students into these roles before they know how to perform them. Or as Vanderslice (2006: 147) suggests 'throwing students like this into the traditional workshop cold is like holding a minnows' swimming lesson in the deep end of the pool'. Rather than go into depth about *how* a story works, the workshop has a history of nitpicking, with students focusing on what they 'like' or 'don't like'. Such personal preferences draw the attention away from the work and towards the reader. More appropriately, 'good writers', R.V. Cassill insists, 'are interested in something more than the application of successful literary formulas, and so they must study texts in addition to principles' (qtd. in Myers, 1994).

Along the same lines, B.W. Jorgensen (Brigham Young University) judges that 'almost no students have a vocabulary for talking about syntax, which seems to be partly why they don't perceive sentences very clearly'.

Jorgensen urges, 'you have to teach them to read like writers; you have to teach them that a sentence is something that can be felt and thought about'.

Whatever the agency behind our students' lack of reading readiness, the workshop model must cultivate the student as literary reader. There is certainly enough substantive information in this section to more than suggest that our students will not be well-read when they enter workshop classes; perhaps, except, in popular genres or as one teacher laments, their 'reading by choice only Anne Rice'. Students' lack of reading history and the lack of literature (reading) courses create an additional load for teachers in the design of their workshop class. Indeed, some teachers, like Lisa Lewis (Oklahoma State), settle the problem of this theory focus in English studies by providing 'a more literary sensibility' for her workshop students. T.R. Hummer (Arizona State University) adds to this position when he says, 'creative writing instructors have to make heroic efforts to make sure their students read enough, and don't assume they can write without reading'. Manning provides another way to reduce this 'additional load', by suggesting we offer courses that intensify reading skills such as a course called 'Reading for Writers', one designed for creative writing students that might stress 'cross genres and literary periods'. Requiring such a course, Manning claims, would then 'add rigor, to a degree, in creative writing'.

Vanderslice (2006: 152) adds to this argument when she reminds us that students also need 'reacquainting ... with the responsibilities of the writing life'. 'These students', she insists, 'need to be introduced to the universe of literary reading and encouraged, perhaps directed, to develop extensive reading lists of authors who might enlarge their sense of the world and their own work'. Assuredly, they need to know how to read as writers, not as literary or composition scholars, whose reading practices differ from ours. Vanderslice suggests that we prepare our students 'to continually ask "why?", to try to get inside the head of the author and "workshop" what they are reading in the same way they might do with a student text' (2006: 152). Creative writers consider the text from the inside, taking into account the effect authors' choices have on a story or poem, to imagine what else a story might be, to conjecture, constructing theories driven by questions of 'What if?'. This, Vanderslice tells us, informs 'the heuristic nature of creative writing to construct for the reader, and for the writer, a hypothesis' (2006: 152).

Such a practice of reading differs from the interpretive function of reading in literary studies, where the interest lies in determining the source of literary texts, the deconstruction of the text (and other more specialized objects of study), which supersedes *how* a story is constructed. R.V. Cassill clarifies our readerly distinction from the determinism of literary studies and the rhetorical modality of composition rhetoric when he insists that '[a]bove all [creative writers] are interested in how texts are *made* – how the parts fit together to form a whole – which means [creative writers] are committed to the view that a text might have been made otherwise than it is' (qtd. in Myers, 1994). The story or poem reads as it does because the author has chosen his or her form from a number of other options. A writer's literary study is situated in this understanding that the writer chooses the story or poetic form. The core of Stephen Tatum's 1993 essay '"The Thing Not Named": The end of creative writing in the English department', which appeared in the *ADE Bulletin*, centered on 'the place or use of theory in an MFA, let alone the PhD degree track in creative writing' and the understanding that 'good writing' should be 'inextricably bound up with "good" critical reading skills'. I review Tatum's 1993 concern in this section because in the wake of that piece, he has since had the opportunity to appreciate the ways in which creative writing students in his critical theory and cultural studies class read theory and criticism 'differently' than his other students and 'how their responses [are] less devoted to, say, themes and arguments per se, and more to thinking about how various critical concepts as well as styles of theoretical writing [are] helpful in articulating' what he refers to as 'craft' decisions. Rather than 'buying in to some narrative about creative writing students regarding theory as "the enemy", or academic colleagues regarding creative writing students on the MFA level as intellectually challenged', Tatum finds himself 'learning both pedagogically and intellectually from some of [his] best creative writing students' ways of reading'. From his creative writing students, Tatum learns 'how to understand some theoretical approaches better through reading contemporary fiction, rather than theoretical approaches coming first and then applied to fiction'[7].

While we know that creative writing students read literature in more specific ways, we also recognize that our students must bear some of the responsibility of expanding their reading range by adding to the bibliographies and reading lists we provide, by seeking out suggested stories, poems and references that might provoke some avenue yet to be developed in their writing. Finally, a scaffolding of writerly-reading courses should be part of the creative writing course design, beginning with basic reading skills to include more intensive reading courses that supplement the workshop model. These protocols further establish the scholar of *creative writing studies* as a discipline markedly different than literary studies and composition studies.

The Case for Writing and its Distinguishing Markers

Creative writers learn to write by reading *and* by writing. We know that reading as a writer is a cognitive process that allows readers to actively process and then manipulate the workings of a text in a manner that is distinct from other kinds of readings. Prose (2006: 9) considers the manner in which works of art trigger thinking from an aesthetic or philosophical perspective. She suggests the reading of a text 'can suggest some new method, some fresh approach to fiction', but she adds that 'the relationship between reading and writing is rarely so clear-cut', relating it to something more active, 'like watching someone dance and then secretly, in your own room, trying out a few steps'.

That the workshop model should demonstrate this link between reading and writing is clear. At the very least, creative writing practice has its roots in early Emersonian construction (as the primary means of literature in the making), compositional practices of invention and modeling and the practice of writing within genres as classified by literary studies. The discipline's writing practice, however, is epistemologically different than those of composition studies and literary studies in that creative writing emphasizes writerly processes, not rhetorical persuasion or philosophical discussions of goals and methods of particular literary camps. Creative writers do not begin with a thesis, a main controlling idea that serves as the contract between writer and reader. Creative writers also do not submit rhetorical modes of persuasion that anticipate the pathos, ethos and logos appeals of our readers. Rarely do creative writers consider opposing views and refutations or contextualize their positions in the larger conversation. They do not organize their stories and poems to resemble the structure of a scholarly essay or argument. Their narration is not laden with the lexicon of academics. Instead, their poems are often fragments, images. In fact, their narrators may be unreliable, the point of view of their stories and poems may be shifting, objective, subjective, omniscient – their diction, perhaps, limited to the confines of a first-person persona.

Rather, from a storytelling perspective, we step inside our characters' minds, showing, perhaps, unique perspectives on ordinary lives. Our characters are flawed, raw, rounded – their lives complicated, convoluted; perhaps, sympathetic – their motives are defined by their movement, dialogue, interactions, the choices they make, the things they ignore. They will change, perhaps ever so subtly through the course of their actions. 'Our fiction', as Robert Olen Butler says, 'is the form of human yearning' (qtd. in Budman, n.d.). We begin in medias res, with an unstable ground situation; perhaps a trigger shifts a story's direction. Creative writers withhold information (or competently control its delivery), diverting off the beaten path if they choose so they may show readers the dust that gathers in the cuff of their character's pants and the grease that collects on the cushy pads of her palms.

Instead of making direct references and connections, readers of creative writing will look for the links, the clues writers drop along the way. Our endings may surprise, rather than summarize, or they may speak to the beginnings of stories or poems. Writers may create atmosphere with their setting – maybe motive, metaphor, believability. They will mix up their narratives – blocks of exposition, summary, direct dialogue, scene breaks – perhaps they will flash forward or backward in time or catapult to new dimensions – other worlds.

The distinction between writing taught and practiced in a creative writing workshop class and writing performed in a composition class has more to do with the compositional practices creative writers must unlearn as they write their poems and stories. Creative writers may have drawn from the composing practices of composition and literary study pedagogies, but clearly, their writing processes are significantly different and marked by their own cognitive theories of writing. What remains is the need for more versatility and experimentation in the workshop writing practice and more studies of its markers of professional differences.

The Case for Responding and its Distinguished Markers

Before addressing student response and distinguishing markers in the creative writing workshop, it is useful to consider what risks and dynamics are at play during the peer review process to the text, the writer, the reader and the teacher. If we are to approach the text as verbal icon in the true fashion of New Criticism, then the text exists in isolation, as words on the paper, never as an incomplete work, but rather, according to Edward White, as a finished product 'in general in order to be criticized' (qtd. in Bizzaro, 1993: 236). Additionally, a New Critical approach becomes complicated because whenever a text is objectified and perceived as final authority, the reading of student work and the workshop dialogue traditionally silences the author, both in the overt discussion of his or her piece and also as it relates to the possible biographical coincidence of the writer to the speaker of a poem or a fictional character in a story. In other words, no authorial intent or biographical nature on social or cultural contextualization embraces or implicates the author. New Criticism's singularly focused reading of the student text does not 'grant to the student possible intentions or insights not yet present on the page' (White qtd. in Bizzaro, 1993: 53).

This approach assumes that students can isolate the words on the page and any interactions with a piece from a social or cultural perspective bears no import on their reading or the usefulness of their feedback. However, Haake reminds us that workshops are not filled with homogenous groups of writers, and this understanding complicates the traditional workshop's narrow reading that is focused on craft and technique. Moreover, the traditional workshop space rarely includes room to challenge master narratives or much maneuverability for the constructs by students which may respond to prevailing literary conventions. A consideration of Mary Louise Pratt's perceptivity in 'Arts of the contact zone' (1999), offers teachers some options in the ways they view and teach within their writing communities to include the way they manage the response component of the workshop model.

In her description of a particular course, one that attracts a diverse body of students, Pratt explains 'how the classroom functioned not like a class of homogenous community or a horizontal alliance, but rather like a contact zone'. Texts at play had historical relationships, and she responds that everyone had a range of stakes in the discourse. This theory has significant implications for the workshop space – a space which also functions as a contact zone. When teachers open the workshop space, flex it, so to speak, then everyone has a stake in the responses of the workshop discussion. There is more movement away from the current limiting workshop response of what works and what does not work according to the personal taste of a particular reader.

Indeed, if we consider, as Pratt does that literate arts of the contact zone include: 'authoethnography, transculturation, critique, collaboration, bilingualism, mediation, imaginary dialogue, parody, and vernacular expression', and that the dangers of writing in the contact zone might create '[m]iscomprehension, incomprehension, dead letters, unread masterpieces, absolute heterogeneity of meaning', then we can better understand that much more is at risk in workshop classes than either composition studies or literary studies when the student text opens to more than just craft. Eugene Garber and Jan Ramjerdi (1994: 14–15) clarify that '[w]hat we are willing to call a response, literary scholars would call an initial personal response which then requires a standing back'. Without such critical distancing, he notes, 'the use of a critical lens turns the text into an object of academic study rather than a nebulous encounter, a blur really, of personal and ideological texts, yours and mine (Hence, more is at stake)' (pp. 14–15).

Healey addresses the need to *'front-load'* workshops with 'interventions in the writing process before it begins and while it is happening', instead of the current practice of 'hammering out literary verdicts like a jury' (Healey, 2009: 38). Grant Matthew Jenkins (University of Tulsa) agrees that when it comes to the workshop setting, the problem lies with 'the competitive, grand-standing nature of the firing-line where the student who is up for critique just absorbs comments from others, who may have ulterior motives for comments'. When students are not taught 'how to put [comments] into practice', one instructor comments, 'the workshop can feel just like "voting" on TV or a focus group'.

Karen Holmberg (Oregon State) wonders if putting 'the writer before the class as a teaching tool' may not be 'ethically problematic'. In addition, the model assumes, as one instructor says, that 'the work under discussion needs "fixing"', like a car brought into the shop for repairs, when, depending on the students' level of seriousness and experience, such an approach may not really be helpful'. However, a number of teachers appreciate how the writer under review in the workshop model prepares students for the kind of feedback and revision practices expected in the community and workforce. Here, the attention is on the purpose of criticism and revising as a means of responsible improvement. J.T. Bushnell (University of Oregon), for example, acknowledges that 'having a story workshopped is uncomfortable for an author' and, as a result, 'more and more writers seem to be responding to this discomfort by rejecting the system that produces it'. His point is that 'writers who reject the workshop experience are the writers who make little or no progress with their work and their vocation'. Bushnell is not alone in this argument. Another surveyed instructor, for instance, concurs that 'even unhealthy dynamics offer teaching moments. It's all about process'. This teacher reminds us that 'student writers of all stripes, from business to science, must learn to show their work around with an eye toward improvement. Civil, sane, and substantive conversations about written work', this teacher insists, 'are essential for a healthy society'.

To continue this line of thought, although the 'pure' workshop, one that 'presumes everyone in the workshop has the ability to read well and to edit in a manner which will help any given individual grow', is 'humanly impossible', states Thom Brucie (Brewton-Parker College), 'a classroom is still a classroom' and 'its efficacy lies in the opportunity to make mistakes and learn from them in an orderly manner, within a short time frame, utilizing a "mentor" to facilitate student learning as much as possible from any given experience'. A well-managed workshop, he contends, presents this classroom experience as one that is 'better than any individual using a singular experience and vast amounts of time in search for answers for problems and vast amounts of time in search of improvement'. Sometimes teachers (and subsequently our students) feel the pressure of this efficacy, of this classroom experience, of this well-managed workshop when they try to cram as much as possible in a single semester with noble intentions to improve our students' work.

Donald Platt (Purdue), however, believes that the '"soul" can easily be sacrificed on the altar of technique', and Peter Harris (Colby College) concludes, if 'workshops privilege clarity', then, perhaps, '[Emily] Dickinson would flunk'. Furthermore, Arielle Greenburg (Columbia College Chicago) rightly suggests that conflicting feedback by 'students – or the professor! – can lead the poet astray or confuse them' because students do not know how to use the workshop comments. For this reason, students might 'validate what is most mediocre or honeyed in the writing, and students may ignore the teacher's criticism because it requires too much work' (Allison Cummings, Southern New Hampshire University). At its worst, one teacher suggests, 'the proliferation of comments serve to dilute student work – certain students try to write the bland story that everyone will kind of think is okay but nobody will love'. McCabe agrees that 'students can be too easily satisfied with the adulation of their peers and not work to make their work as strong as it could be'. To add further confusion, the opposite may hold true in that students learn to disregard their peers' comments if they run contrary to the writer's intentions or they dismiss all comments but the teacher's as exemplary reader of their work, the one who assigns it, finally, a grade. This notion gives Martin Cockroft (Waynesburg University) pause to speculate 'if Rilke was right: Critical response to creative work results in "happy misunderstandings", rather than clarity, increased range, or aesthetic growth'. He reminds us that Donald Hall wrote that 'our contemporary poetry will be remembered for its mediocrity and lack of ambition'. He wonders if the workshop model, the way it 'helps churn out the same "workshop" writing – a poem mill, doesn't contribute to this'.

It is clearly this derisive naming of what is wrong with a piece, the focus on the end product (though revision is intended) and the inconstancy of a reader's agency that ascribes such negativity to the workshop model. There is so much room for improvement in this process. For starters, the beginning creative writer who is still exploring the 'writerly' and 'readerly' processes of creative writing cannot be expected to evaluate a body of work with any critical wisdom. This ability requires not only the diligence of study and practice, but much reading experience and an ability to approach a body of work from a consonant perspective. This is certainly not an endorsement to abolish the workshop at this level, as students can still benefit from, at the very least, having an audience for their work. Rather, it is a caveat that too early immersion into a workshop process can lead to unhelpful critiques, premature inflation of writing ability or an early censor of a still-burgeoning piece.

Even at the MFA and PhD level the workshop can create a good deal of guarding and gainsaying. This causes Philip Gerard to be decidedly tepid on regarding the traditional workshop as the ultimate pedagogical tool. What he says is an argument echoed by many in the field, but it is worth trumpeting the horn one more time: 'It can be a lot of people sitting around', he insists, 'saying "I liked this but I didn't like that"', and it can do more harm than good by creating a lot of defensiveness' (qtd. in Delaney, 2007). Student responses such as these are not only *not* helpful to the writer or the piece or to the collective learning experience of the class, but they remain superficial and do not help creative writers to distinguish markers of professional difference in the ways creative writing students respond to written work differently than composition studies and literary studies. On the other end of the spectrum, creative writers – especially some beginning undergraduate writers – can be a quiet group. How do we get them responding to any kind of writing? Students who write together in class, share their works and talk about the act of writing, share experiences that build knowledge and trust. Perry (2010: 110) refers to this practice as the *'hands-on writing workshop'* – a space where 'students write in response to triggers in the form of writing exercises' – a place where '[w]e talk and write, write and talk' – where they 'tend to generate writing that is more exploratory and less predictable'. So when students do come to Perry's peer-review workshop, 'the act of writing is not removed from the more formal drafts produced even though they are usually prepared out of site of the class' (2010: 118). Both spaces create dynamics and energy that are often not experienced in other academic disciplines – because writing and responding to writing is performative – and this practice of our art form demonstrates another professional marker of difference.

I am in agreement with those who advocate for another version of the workshop, one that does not privilege identity as defined or voice as singular or workshop writing as finite. Let me emphasize that such a workshop is possible. There are new spaces to construct for the workshop model: spaces that 'dismantle authority' and consider what more the model can offer. Haake (2005: 99) tells us when she first recognized the repetitive cadence in her voice, 'to hear [herself] tell the same stories, say the same things'. Her aim became 'to disorient students sufficiently so as to force them into a new space for writing' (2005: 100). As a result, she developed topics-based writing seminars and hybrid workshops, 'products of intensive scholarly rigor and careful planning' (2005: 101).

Yet there is still more to be done. Light's provocative new understanding of students' conceptions of *voice* and Healey's advice that we question the authenticity of *voice* are markers that must give us pause to reconsider our thinking and our practice. This is not to suggest that ideologies will not be challenged or that writers will not acquiesce to the majority rule in creative writing workshops. Rather, Healey suggests that instead of competition, that 'we learn through collaboration, as members of a group that collectively encounters a series of writing tasks and critical activities, that studies past and present models, all with judgment suspended (Healey, 2009: 38). This is not composition's version of collaborative theory in which consensus risks individualization, but rather, one I perceive as open dialogue, one in which the process of writing is our driving compulsion. In an environment in which the variable ways that writers might approach a text and the variable ways that writers might be influenced in their writing are interesting points of departure from old traditions of what is working, followed quickly by what needs fixing. Moreover, discussions get interesting when a written piece (professional- or student-generated) rubs against students' ideology. These are useful opportunities for expanded discussions, intriguing encounters to discuss processes of writing.

Eugene Garber (Garber & Ramjerdi, 1994: 17) adds to this argument when he talks about the limits of discussion that go so far, that 'don't really get to the profound cultural, epistemological, maybe even ontological works that appear to be representational but don't represent correctly (e.g. re-represent the master narratives)'. He believes that conversations that head in this direction 'will be the most energetic because people will see that the counters and structures of master narratives are really being challenged' (p. 17). While we don't need to turn the creative writing workshop into a forum for social or political agendas, there are refreshing opportunities for the discipline to shift the workshop tenor from its current default mode of finding fault to addressing the writerly process of what choices a writer makes and *how* those choices affect the reading of the work.

Mayers (2005) shares an anecdote regarding an undergraduate workshopping of his poem and how it was revised based on that experience. His motivation for the retelling is to wonder what might have happened instead. For the most part, the workshop discussion focused on the elements of craft – overall it was more of an editing, rather than revision focus. 'Perhaps, the most interesting avenues of discussion about the poem', Mayers shares, 'were implied in the professor's seemingly off-the-cuff remarks before we moved on to the next poem' (p. 141). Mayers recalls the professor pausing, with a glance back to his poem before offering to Mayers that on his first read, he 'half expected to hear a jazz saxophone in the background', supposing that 'some people might think of this kind of poem as high art' (p. 141). Because Mayers' workshop space was closed off to discussions such as what kinds of imagery and topoi might have been generated by the professor's association, Mayers' revision was limited to simple technique rather than a discussion of what else was possible. In this respect then we can envision how our writing community 'can help students better understand how language is a social force, and how their writing practice functions in a social context' (Healey, 2009: 38).

The Case for Creative Writing Research as Knowledge

The case for creative writing research as knowledge can be categorized in terms of what we know and what we don't know about creative writing research and knowledge.

What We Know about Creative Writing Research and Knowledge

At the 2011 AWP conference, panelists of one session presented the survey results of attendees' views on research practices in creative writing. The panel, comprised predominantly of creative writing practitioners from the United Kingdom, was surprised that the overall survey response indicated a relative apathy by creative writers in the area of research. If we infer that responders were predominantly American writers and teachers, then the indifference to research in the creative writing domain can be explained through a juxtaposition of creative writing in the United States with programs situated in the United Kingdom and Australian universities.

For one, while UK and Australian graduate students complete both a creative dissertation and a substantial critical essay (of which the latter contributes to disciplinary knowledge), the creative dissertation in the United States ('still conceived as a literary work to be circulated outside the academy') (Earnshaw, 2007: 87), is recognized as the Masters or doctoral academic equivalency of research output. In fact, in the UK and Australia, the creative dissertation counts as research only when it is associated with a valid work of research. This hybridization of creative and critical considers not only the processes of creative writers in action, but also 'an original investigation undertaken in order to gain knowledge and understanding' (Candy, 2006). In other words, the 'creative work acts as a form of research' in that the creative practice – 'the training and specialized knowledge that creative practitioners have and the processes they engage in when they are [writing a creative piece]' – leads to 'specialised research insights which can then be generalised and written up as research' (Smith & Dean, 1988: 5). Hazel Smith and Roger T. Dean (1988: 5) explain that '[t]he first argument [*practice-based research*] emphasises creative practice in itself, while the second [*practice-led research*] highlights the insights, conceptualisation and theorisation which can arise when [writers] reflect on and document their own creative practices'.

Secondly, university regulations and the expectations of the academy steer research practices in the UK and in Australia, and the agencies behind these regulations and expectations are government funding bodies. In contrast, there is no funding impetus for the United States to design practice-led research programs as part of graduate creative writing study. As a further deterrent, little professional impulsion exists at the academic level for creative writing teachers to engage in the critical study of creative writing. In fact, Moxley (2010: 231) places 'the constraining force of the existing faculty reward system' in perspective when he indicates not only 'how slow the discipline is to evolve', but how his groundbreaking scholarly 1989 collection *Creative Writing in America: Theory and Pedagogy* did not count toward his tenure. Add to this limitation the didactic nature of staggering 2010–2011 student enrollment numbers with major university 'cut-backs' on faculty hires and increased undergraduate class size (25–90 students per class) and *time* becomes a valued commodity for writer-teachers to pursue only those creative works that advance their promotion portfolios. Moreover, while there is movement toward exploring creative writing practice in the United States, the discipline remains more pedagogical than critical and theoretical in its approach. Whereas, creative writing teachers might examine teaching pedagogies in their scholarship and/or at conference forums and while these theorizations might influence – to some degree – their teaching practices (and those, perhaps, of conference attendees), their graduate students at the academy do not critically study their writing processes by joining their creative work with critical exigeses that offer new knowledge to the field of study. Creative writing in the United States, situated within a research facility, remains estranged from other disciplines that actively engage in research. It is still considered the softer discipline, the angelic community on university and college campuses.

While there remain some concerns about defining creative writing research methods and integrating creative writing research to fit existing academic protocols in the UK and Australia-based PhD programs, creative writing programs in these countries do position graduates to consider critical theory in congruence with their creative work early in their higher education experience. As a result, UK and Australian graduate students contribute (and are expected to contribute) to their universities' research practices, shaping the study of creative writing, as they do, as a research discipline. As such, research in creative writing becomes an increasingly important aspect of the university's productivity as well as an increasingly important aspect to the development of creative writing research as knowledge.

If we talk about research in the United States, it is more in line with Michael Meehan's (2010) intentional 'disguise ... [of] anything like research has ever taken place'. While '[a]cademic writing foregrounds research', Meehan tells us, creative writing still requires 'a huge amount of research, not just in gathering information but in gathering texture; that is, in putting together the kind of information you need to create an "insider" sense of foreign, unfamiliar, past or future environments'. The kind of research that benefits the development and credibility of the creative work, however, is not the same as practice-led research that 'is directed towards knowledge more generally to increasing the store of humanity's knowledge' (Candy, 2006).

Additionally, when we talk about the growth of United States postgraduate degrees in creative writing, we understand that we're not referring to new theoretical frameworks or adding critical exigeses to the PhD program at this time or even discerning, as the Australian National Association of Writers in Education (NAWE) does, that *undergraduate* creative writing 'is more akin to "scholarship" (where knowledge is developed and applied but does not necessarily involve new insights) and *postgraduate* creative writing is more akin to "research" (where new knowledge, new insights, and new discoveries are the primary focus' (NAWE, italics mine). In the United States, the relation of creative writing to knowledge is through program design in the (1) 'systematic teaching of skills employed by writers which are equivalent or analogous to those of scholarly research' (Earnshaw, 2007: 87) and to a lesser degree (2) in the preparation of Masters and doctoral students to teach new skills to undergraduates. In the United States the relation of creative writing to knowledge is through the field's growing body of pedagogy and knowledge. Anna Leahy (Day et al., 2011) considers the body of knowledge in creative writing as the 'equivalent of theory', though she admits calling this knowledge 'theory' is 'tricky' as creative writing is a 'practice discipline', of which some is 'pedagogical, some verges on "how to"', and some is akin to literary scholarship'.

Creative writing in the UK higher education institutions has departed from practice-based models. Creative writing research in the UK may have begun 'with basic notions connected to knowledge, knowledge investigation and knowledge acquisition', but creative writing research now 'proceeds by the recognition of the evidence for both empirical and theoretical research' (Harper, 2008: 164–5). In Australia, the creative work joins a critical composition that blends theory and practice. The creative work 'is accompanied by an exegesis placing the artifact within a body of scholarly knowledge and hence acting to bring together theory and practice in a hybrid thesis format aimed at a variety of audiences' (Kroll, 2004). Prior to 1996 creative writing had 'no research activity [or peak body] by which it could identify itself' (Krauth, 2000). However, the Australian Association of Writing Programs (now known as the Australasian Association of Writing Programs to reflect writing programs in New Zealand and Asia) and the Research in the Creative Arts Project helped to catapult Australia's later development in creative writing research in tertiary institutions. The model comes from a change in the way the Australian government evaluates research performance in Australian universities. In brief, the 2009 Excellence in Research for Australia (ERA) initiative 'included – for the first time – assessment of creative works as research' (Carey et al., 2008: 2) and grouped creative writing with theater and music disciplines as part of a research category called Studies in Creative Arts and Writing. In addition, the 2010 ERA trial program required the creative writing discipline (as part of the creative arts and writing track) to 'pinpoint what exactly about their work constitutes research and is an original contribution to knowledge' (Hecq & Banagan, 2010).

Research and new understanding are linked in both the UK and Australian graduate creative writing programs. The 2008 NAWE benchmarks stipulate that 'contextualization, reflection on, or response to the creative text forms part of the research and the final thesis'.[8] Moreover, this contextualization and reflection should advance new knowledge in the creative writing discipline. More specifically, some of the following are highly relevant to the postgraduate project:

- The presence, or absence, of an original contribution to creative writing as a discipline.
- The level of inventiveness, and the qualities of authenticity and innovation evident in the process and/or results.
- The creative writer's engagement with their subject matter, formal development and/or with genre or audience awareness.
- The degree of displayed competence with regard to the textual and/or inter-textual strategies employed.
- The fitness of research strategies that have been in place in the undertaking of the work.
- The level of effectiveness of the completed work or works. (NAWE, 2008)

As such, students balance practice and theory and '[j]ustify [this] process and theory in their hybrid thesis', all of which 'requires reflexibility, creativity and experimentation as well as scholarship' (Kroll, 2009: 10).

While funding imperatives and university requirements do not compel the United States discipline to integrate practice-led research into their programs, there is still a cogent and persuasive rationale for investigating and discovering practices that will reveal new modes of knowledge to the writer and to the discipline. Convincing practitioners in the United States that practice-led research has merit, however, means answering such questions as: 'How might we clarify the relation of creative writing to "knowledge" and consider what we mean by "research"?' (Harper, 2008: 164). The simple answer is that research offers 'an opportunity to develop as creators and to produce more satisfactory work' (Scrivener, 2000: 4). Steven Scrivener (2000: 50), who is familiar with supervising and examining PhD projects, shows us the value in the actions and reflections of a creative and critical postgraduate study as a process that 'is inventive and imaginative, and realised through and in artefacts'. One of the principle underlying theories of research is that it offers a way of making new meaning through reflection. In the UK and Australian creative writing programs, graduate students who approach their creative and critical journey are guided 'to be conscious not only of process ... but context, looking backward in order to look forward – to perceive, in effect, what needs to be done creatively at this point in their culture' (Kroll, 2008: 9). It's a recursive process in which research 'begins before-during/after practice, aided by ideas generated by practice, in order to produce new knowledge' (Kroll, 2008: 9). The process incorporates a research question at the onset (or early in the process) of writing creatively, so that the critical exploration intersects at many points with the creative process. Most importantly, the research that defines the hybrid thesis is not a personal reflection of what the writer learns about herself through the process of writing, but rather one that investigates the process, the genre and/or the discipline and results in the contribution of original (new) knowledge to the field of study.

Significantly, research leads to creative writing as knowledge and, as teachers, we should want, at the least, to be informed about our pedagogy. Leahy concurs that '[a]s long as we are teaching, we remain responsible for articulating not just what we do but also how and why we teach the way we do' (Day et al., 2011). Creative writing in the United States moves forward in this pedagogical reflection in small measures through its publications and presentations that probe creative writing practices and processes. Research into our processes and practices lead us to consider what else is possible in the workshop space, to suggest how we might best assess student writing and to embrace (among others) multimodal approaches and new conceptual spaces for digital compositions.

These pedagogical movements, which are more practice-based than experiential, inch the discipline forward in incremental steps. If the attendance at the 2011 AWP pedagogy session is any indication of the interest many writers now have in practice-based creative writing research, then we can hope for more opportunities to shape creative writing as knowledge.

We begin with the AWP conference pedagogy forums (and others such as creative writing forums at the CCCC conferences), along with print and online publications, to advance new theories and practice that help to create an intellectual global community that learns from the research of the field. Jeri Kroll (2004) reminds us that '[i]n order for writers to understand their place in the culture ... they must understand – as scientists must – what else is being done' in the field. The United States attends to this understanding as its major writing conferences bring together important discussions and research in the discipline. Scrivener (2000) suggests that '[i]n general, practitioners are not simply focused on practice: they look at and read about the work of others, they read professional and (sometimes) academic journals and monitor social, cultural and scientific development'. US writer-teachers invest time in the kind of professional development Scrivener addresses but there remains little activity at the university level that combines this knowledge acquisition activity with on-site opportunities to 'uncover [the] new theory and knowledge' that 'runs parallel to practice' (Scrivener, 2000). *Creative writing studies*, as an academic discipline, might bring more of this wider practice-based research to the university program level as well as develop portals for the kind of practice-led research that leads to new discoveries. From a programmatic level, there would need to be significant architectural and philosophical changes to the US creative writing programs to add a critical exigesis to its post-graduate program. But until this hybrid thesis can be (or should be) added, creative-critical-writer-teachers might complement the discipline's current scholarship and pedagogy in small measures to include more training of graduate creative writing students in the history and practice of the field. The critical reflections that would develop as a result of such efforts could then establish new patterns of research inquiry and new understandings and insights. *Creative writing studies* as an academic discipline supports creativity as 'the ability to come up with ideas or artefacts that are *new, surprising and valuable*' (Boden 2004: 1). Inquiries into the creative writing process and field add knowledge to our discipline, and such knowledge acquisition would translate to new theories and new skills to teach to our students.

Adding creative writing research to the US creative writing program design will lead to more operational significance for our practice.

What We Don't Know/Need to Know about Creative Writing Research and Knowledge

What we need to know is how creative writing research can effectively be benchmarked and measured. But before we explore how best to benchmark and measure such research, we need to understand why we should consider such efforts. John Grech, who 'focuses on the interactive, dialogic nature of creative practice', notes that '[t]he way that creative work and practice-led research become verifiable is to measure their effect within and through discourse' (qtd. in Perry, 2008: 7). Additionally, while we know that 'creative writing research methodology exists', we don't know how to articulate these methods quite yet as we've not yet begun to explore them in any significant context.[9] Academic creative writing programs in the UK and Australia have a repository of data that supports creative writing research as knowledge. Through supervisions and examinations of PhD projects and explorations of research methods and benchmark language, these programs might advance a more global understanding of how creative writing can contribute knowledge to the academy and the field.

What we need to know about creative writing and research is how to facilitate a better understanding of creative writing's particular modes of research. While academic research methodologies have been clearly defined, creative writing 'needs to develop its own domain-specific methodologies' (Dean & Smith, 2006: 5). With full control of its own research methods, the discipline should define 'under what conditions meaning is to be treated as knowledge or as the acquisition of knowledge' (Niklas Luhmann qtd. in Reilly, 2002) rather than to have these conditions awkwardly shaped by traditional university research standards. As creative writing researchers we need 'to promote a better understanding of where our particular kind of activity "fits", and to claim appropriate support for our high productivity in this area' (Meehan, 2010).

While creative writing programs in the US are not at the same level as practice-led research as the UK and Australia, writers and writer-teachers at national and international writing association conferences (AWP, AAWP, NAWE, Great Writing: the International Creative Writing Conference) can attest to there now being 'a strongly developing body of understanding about the nature of creative writing, and considerable articulation of the nature of creative writing research, its knowledge base and understanding' (Harper, 2008: 161). One organization that promotes this global community and undertakes research through the activity of creative writing as well as through critical examination of creative writing practice is the International Center for Creative Writing Research (ICCWR).[10] *Creative writing studies* as an academic discipline can encourage practitioners to link theory with practice and to form its own creative writing theory. As this is possible, 'we' (defined as a collective international voice) can agree to treat research 'as an activity which can appear in a variety of guises across the spectrum of practice and research' (Muecke, 2010: 3), so that the significance of what creative writing as a global field has to offer moves beyond our international program degree differences to a communal space in which a common 'global' language might exist from which to talk about creative writing as knowledge.

The Workshop Model: Final Arguments

The writing workshop stays the same when workshop teachers continue to produce 'their own interpretations of creative writing classroom lore in a field that as a whole rejects notions of itself as an academic discipline' (Ritter & Vanderslice, 2007: xi). Most of us do not want to replicate the tired workshop model, despite Starkey's claim that much is at stake for some in maintaining the status quo. Johns Hopkins program director Jean McGarry warns, 'If workshops are only about self-expression, then you have literary bums floating in and out' (qtd. in Delaney, 2007). Teachers who promote rigor and inventiveness in the workshop model stretch the model's flexibility – and in doing so, they also shape, for the better, our pedagogy, our students and our profession as an intelligent model set apart in its distinctiveness from composition studies and literary studies.

Notes

1. Portions of this section appear in my introduction to the edited 2010 collection *Does the Writing Workshop Still Work?*, Multilingual Matters.
2. Included in my text are comments/quotes by creative writing teachers who responded to my survey on the workshop model. To best distinguish these responses from other cited scholarship, I have identified the feedback from surveyed creative writing teachers with in-text parentheses that note responders' names and universities.
3. This was a concept introduced by Irwin Colin in a preliminary essay for my 2010 collection *Does the Writing Workshop Still Work?*
4. See http://www.bangor.ac.uk/creative_industries/
5. See http://www.qut.edu.au/

6. See Columbia University's School of the Arts website at http://www.columbia.edu/cu/writing/, Florida State University website at http://www.english.fsu.edu/crw/index.html, NYU website at http://cwp.fas.nyu.edu/page/lillianvernonhouse, Michener Center for Writers at the University of Texas at Austin website at http://www.utexas.edu/academic/mcw/, Chatham University website at http://www.chatham.edu/mfa/.
7. R.S. Tatum (personal communications, May 11, 2011).
8. See http://www.nawe.co.uk/writing-in-education/writing-at-university/research.html and click on the CW Benchmarks.pdf
9. This suggestion comes from my December 2010 Skype conversation with Graeme Harper.
10. The International Center for Creative Writing Research (ICCWR) is headed by Graeme Harper at http://www.iccwr.org.

SECTION 3

The Academic Home of *Creative Writing Studies*

Control of Space, Domain and Power

The Academic Home of *Creative Writing Studies*

The Academic Home of *Creative Writing Studies*

Perhaps the first objective in determining the academic home of *creative writing studies* would be one of purpose. Earlier, I positioned creative writing at a crossroads along with *creative writing studies*. In my discussion of the workshop model, I speculated on the trajectories of both disciplines and recommended course development, program designs and curricular tracks at the undergraduate and graduate levels. In this section, I argue for the academic home for *creative writing studies*. It should be noted, however, that as I consider the space for *creative writing studies* in the academy, the academic residence of the discipline of creative writing (perhaps in a more dimensional form) becomes a natural part of the discussion. This crossover occurs primarily because creative writing has a history and relationship with the institution and with the disciplines of English studies and because *creative writing studies* is an emergent field.

    I submit that given the value-added service that creative writing provides to the academy, there are a number of location options for the discipline of creative writing, one of which is to remain within the English department as a viable and growing program for students whose first priority is to write. At the very least, as I explore placement options for *creative writing studies* as my primary aim in this section, there arise many opportunities for creative writing to add more dimension to its field. As *creative writing studies* stands at the crossroads, it does so with what I suggest is a keener vantage point. Its orientation permits a far-reaching view of where the discipline of creative writing has been, and as best as the practitioners of *creative writing studies* can judge from the topography below, what might lie ahead for their students, their profession and their field.

    Why, if creative writing is such a popular program housed mostly in English departments do we need to consider the academic home of *creative writing studies*? Could *creative writing studies* not just set up its scholarly operations from the current home base of creative writing? Further, to draw creative writing into this discussion and to assert an academic home for *creative writing studies* means drudging up considerable unrest. We must grapple with the voices of contention from literary critics who appreciate what our student numbers mean to their own discipline, not the least of which is more students reading literature. Then there are the concerns of compositionists who identify with our 'underdog' status and the constructivist aims in our writing classes. But any talk of an academic home for *creative writing studies* also means some heel digging from our own creative writing teachers, many of whom dislike much delving into their practices and who, perhaps, want to keep the mystery and lore in and around the process of writing, and who, generally, resist reform. Why provoke such a discussion? After all, an argument can be made (in American universities) that creative writing now represents one of the three major 'power blocks' in the English department, along with literary studies and composition studies. Creative writing's rising course and program enrollments certainly suggest it has arrived as an academic discipline. As long as these numbers climb, creative writing could invariably carry on its operations, its workshop-centered classrooms.

In a sense, creative writing's academic home has been a point in question since Emerson pledged for a democratization of creative power and a desire to study creative writing within American universities. It took 50 years for Emerson's vision of creative writing in the academy to take place, however construed it was (in its purity) as an opposition to philology's scientific study of literature. Conceived later as a pedagogy, creative writing operated as a studio-based model at the University of Iowa, then its writers and poets soon attended the same faculty meetings as did literary critics and composition scholars. Richard Hugo's (1979: 54) reasoning seems cogent when he says, '[t]he English department seemed a logical place for creative writing perhaps because it was already involved with other writing, critical and expository ... and the assumption that reading and writing was closely related'.

Although creative writing programs continue to develop and student enrollment steadily rises, the discipline remains divergent from the scholarly norm within English studies. Shirley Geok-lin Lim (2003: 154) speaks of the 'major oddness of creative writing', how its forms of poetry, fiction and drama shape 'the chief substance of what is studied and taught', how it is largely absent from the history of literary studies despite its pivotal role, and how it is 'hardly visible as a disciplinary component of the profession'. While much of this history and pedagogy is different in the UK and in Australia, creative writing programs in the United States 'have seldom received the scrutiny of outsiders or been required to account for themselves to the same extent as programs like composition and American studies'

(Lim, 2003: 156). Lim asks 'How does the modern research university incorporate or contain creative writing?' (p. 151).

Today, creative writing graduates compete for many of the same jobs as their rhetoric and composition and literary studies counterparts. Mixed course loads that include the teaching of creative writing, creative nonfiction, modern literature and composition coursework are the norm, particularly in liberal arts colleges and academic environments where versatility impacts the bottom line. Theory-based PhD creative writing candidates, specifically present with more multi-faceted attractiveness than ever before. These candidates join with MFA graduates; both groups have received little to no teacher preparation in creative writing. As a result, creative writing graduates join the majority of faculty in their field who do not know their history or theories that underpin their pedagogy. Teachers are less likely to inquire or research or publish scholarship on topics related to their field, and they are inclined to follow the tradition of the workshop model. Our student numbers may have increased, but the development of our pedagogy has not kept pace.

I argue for a different kind of space for *creative writing studies*, an academic home that occupies more substance for the discipline, more equal-but-separate-standing with its colleagues in literary studies and composition studies, and more distinction for its students. My research question in this section asks: What *space* will give *creative writing studies* more meaning for the academy, for its profession and for its student body so that it might fully avail itself of the qualities needed for the best representation as a scholarly field?

Control of Space, Domain and Power

Foucault argues that 'space is fundamental in any form of communal life; space is fundamental in any exercise of power' (qtd. in Porter & Sullivan, 1993: 389). With this in mind, relations of power, knowledge and space become entwined, unavoidable. Foucault also tells us that space is a vital part of the battle for control, of which power can be productive and negative. Territorial disputes ordinarily ensue in this struggle because of competing ideologies and the subsequent control of space, domain and power. We see these power dynamics play out in what has been a mostly hegemonic English department in which literary studies has occupied the terrain, and thus the power. In the seventies and eighties, in particular, not only did literary studies have a poor view of the intellectual contribution of creative writing faculty, but teachers of creative writing (mostly MFA graduates) often held a dim view of their *own* desire to participate in the writing of literary criticism and/or the study/practice of theory. Certainly, as creative writing and literary studies situated under one umbrella, friction ensued. Creative writers were not taken seriously then, and today – with the rise of PhD creative writing programs – some literature professors continue to perceive such programs and their creative dissertation as anti-intellectual.

While *space* can be a theater of operation for such power dynamics, Foucault also posits space as a space of freedom, as unconstrained by barriers. It is within this idealized space of freedom that I wish to springboard my argument that *creative writing studies* must secure its academic home and its separate-but-equal position to that of literary studies and composition studies. It's hard to argue for a physical space for *creative writing studies* because the creative writing discipline is housed in many different location on campus. Creative writing programs in the United States, in particular, are situated within English departments, but this is not always the case. Vanderslice reminds us 'that the role of creative writing varies from institution to institution, from a general education requirement at some schools that encompasses thousands of students, to a small single course requiring instructor position to enroll ... We shouldn't talk of the field as if it's uniform throughout' (Day *et al.*, 2011), and that variability implies that there will be physical location disparities as well. And on the issue of disparity, it is of interest that creative writing programs span across many different department and building locations that range from communication departments to English departments to Fine Arts and other Creative Arts departments. While there are physical options for *creative writing studies*, the conceptual space of creative writing as an academic discipline – its intellectual environment, its epistemological differences from other subjects and its contribution to the academy and to its field – is even more important than the physical location of *creative writing studies* within the institution.

The Academic Home of *Creative Writing Studies*

Here I explore the fronts which have come forward in their architectural plan for creative writing and *creative writing studies* – either with an offer for creative writing to *coexist* within English studies or as a separatist consortium apart from the department of English. In the end, I argue against these offers as the *primary* home for *creative writing studies*. I petition, instead, for an academic home for *creative writing studies* that stands on more equitable ground, that promotes the visibility (rather than the isolation) of its practitioners, that incorporates graduate career training to include teacher preparation, that articulates its research agenda and academic forums and that permits its practitioners to claim *creative writing studies* as a research area. While exploring its academic home, my argument promotes *creative writing studies* as a convincing professional body of knowledge.

Creative Writing Studies and Literary Studies

In her 2006 president's column of the *MLA Newsletter*, Marjorie Perloff speculates on the growing number of PhD creative writing programs and what such a rise in development will mean for literary studies. She concludes that PhD creative writing graduates will be asked to teach, in addition to creative writing classes, a modern literature course or two. Conjointly, this candidate will be expected to have some 'knowledge of early literary periods, genres and conventions as well as of the present', if one considers the traditional required curriculum of a graduate student's literature coursework (2006: 4). Since logic presents that PhD-level creative writing faculty will incorporate theories of reading as well as 'the study of rhetoric – the *how* of writing rather than the *what*' (Perloff, 2006: 4) in their pedagogical approaches to teaching, these practices correlate, for those in literary studies, as more engagement by students in the reading of literature. For Perloff and others, what unites PhD creative writing graduates (not all of which will teach in the academy) is the 'love for the field of human interest' – the field of literature – 'a field without which creative writing could not exist and which, conversely, may currently have no other place to go' (p. 4).

The above explanation is necessary to appreciate the ties (whether positive or not) that bind creative writing to literary studies. In this case, the perception exists for those like Perloff that creative writing requires literature as a means of teaching its students, and the reading of literature has always been considered a hierarchal function of literary studies. On the other hand, this insight also suggests that the important new work in the field of *creative writing studies* combined with the noticeable decline of 20th century literature, may mean that the discipline of literary studies may have 'no other place to go' than to creative writing. It seems clear that literary studies would desire to maintain propriety over creative writing because 'creative writing was perceived by many to belong with literature and the reception of texts' (Crow & O'Neil, 2002: 31). The antecedent of such a view that creative writing's role is to acquaint students to literature can be found in the early 20th century laboratory school where Hugh Mearns' students were introduced to literature as a means of permitting their experimentation with it.

Along the same lines as Perloff, Paul Dawson (2005) buttresses the partnership between creative writing and literary studies. He redefines a role for creative writing in his formation of literary studies in what he refers to as 'the New Humanities'. While Dawson's view vilifies Perloff's dramatization of the struggles between writers and critics over the integrity of literature or the importance of aesthetic value, he nonetheless sees the common ground and common goal between creative writing and literary studies as one based on a vision of social agency rather than a theory of generic form or of the creative process.

Dawson, personally attuned to the potential offered by Australian creative writing programs in the post-Theory environment of the 'New Humanities', collapses the writer and critic into the figure of the public intellectual – 'the exemplary figure of the New Humanities' (2005: 201). Dawson outlines the various forms of literary authority assumed by the writer and shows how this authority has positioned the writer (2005: 185), and he seeks another purpose for creative writing 'beyond its "official" purpose of employing and training writers' (2005: 192). There must be, Dawson argues 'a function specific to the university', that would 'contribute to the domain of knowledge of cultural intellectuals within the academy by the provision of a literary education' (2005: 192). As such, rather than continue 'the teaching of writing literature alongside the teaching of writing criticism', Dawson argues for a particular 'mode of literary research within the academy', one which would entail 'literary and critical writing as complementary practices' (2005: 178–179).

While I support the creative writer role as public intellectual and appreciate the benefits of joining forces in the best interest of serving the academy and agree to the complement of literary (creative) and critical writing, Dawson's view limits other avenues which *creative writing studies* might pursue if it were to more appropriately direct its own pursuits. For example, the use of social media in *creative writing studies* is one such path that might obscure traditional literature readings by virtue of its immediacy and technology. If we are to become a place where students can generate ideas, try out these new ideas and continue a quest for human expression, if we consider that 'writing spaces' influence what we write and how we interact with others, then we might also want to collaborate with others in the fields of media and technology to explore – in our courses and program design – options of digital writing and digital teaching. This hybridity opens spaces for learning across interfaces, creating more intellectual spaces/virtual spaces. These kinds of forward-thinking vehicles of creation might very well go against the grain of literary studies' more traditional modes of instruction.

To add to my argument against such an academic home for *creative writing studies*, it is not certain how such a partnership (or collapse) might affect decision-making or shape the program development for creative writers at the undergraduate and graduate level. Who speaks for the goals and direction of creative writing programs and the development of *creative writing studies* and their students in such a 'partnership'? How does Dawson's 'New Humanities' offer markers of professional difference for our field? To take on a collective academic identity under the umbrella of 'New Humanities' steers us away from our approaching identity as writers and artists *and* teachers and scholars. Such uncertainty adds to a familiar unease concerning the dominance of literary studies over the discipline of creative writing. Furthermore, it seems doubtful that this new academic home might incorporate a negotiation between the ways in which texts are interpreted and literature is studied, a fundamental difference between literary studies and creative writing and *creative writing studies*. As such, refiguring a new discipline in this space seems implausible given the unlikely shift in the current structural model of English studies. Moreover, collapsing the creative writer and the literary critic, as Dawson suggests, can be accomplished in the same person, without the consociation of literary studies – in the field of *creative writing studies*, we call this person a 'craft critic' (Mayers, 2005).

Creative Writing Studies and Cultural Studies

The argument for locating *creative writing studies* within the cultural studies program is tied to the idea of an all-round aesthetic education for our students. Such an aesthetic education proves problematic in an English department in which literary studies splinters into a variety of movements, most centered on the ideological or historical analysis of a text and in which creative writing focuses mostly on writerly processes and the production of a well-formed piece of work. The debate for an academic home for *creative writing studies* within cultural studies predicates that a union between *creative writing studies* and cultural studies is the answer to the known divide between creative writing and literary studies. Such a divide is more than territorial if the methodology for approaching writing within an arts curriculum encourages what Peter Howarth (2007: 41) refers to as 'doublethink in its students'. In other words, students 'code-switch' depending on the class they are in, and this reflects the split within the academy between those who theorize (critics) and those who produce poems and stories (writers).

Rather than encourage such a split, proponents believe that making creative writing or *creative writing studies* part of a cultural studies program will narrow the gap between creative freedom and historical criticism. Students would, perhaps, resist the traditional critical evaluation of a work and instead reflect upon the felt experience of reading and/or writing a particular form. Coursework might include literary theory, medieval literature and sociolinguistics along with parallel seminars in which creative readings guide discussions of cultural categories that resist or oblige those which students encounter in their reading and/or writing. Such integration with cultural studies leads Kevin Brophy (2000: 203) to conclude this synthesis is critical 'if creative writing students are to maintain a level of sophistication and security important to resisting rigidity in their approaches to writing'. In addition to advancing a more aesthetic education for our students, the rationale behind linking *creative writing studies* with cultural studies is to reconcile the kind of split thinking that the traditional English studies curriculum promotes for students engaged in both literary studies criticism and creative writing.

It is hard to dispute any programmatic depth that would add a series of practical cultural studies courses and seminar discussions as a means of facilitating students' experience of *creative writing studies* to the social contexts of literary criticism. Undergraduate and graduate programs should, of course, involve students in a course of study that introduces them to a score of possibilities. However, to pursue the development of *creative writing studies* as an academic discipline to this end would mean limiting *creative writing studies* in this singular focus.

Creative Writing Studies and Independent Writing Programs

The academic home for *creative writing studies* in an independent writing program assumes a unique configuration of space quite different from what – for the discipline of creative writing – remains on the fringes of the English department. This space would not be a part of an English studies department, but rather it would stand apart as a newly-formed disciplinary space devoted exclusively to writing. Such a space comes also with the need to negotiate many more bureaucratic and operational issues such as funding, staffing, curriculum and questions of how such an independent writing program would gain acceptance within the existing structures of universities.

If we are to appraise the 'new kinds of collaborations', along with opportunities for 'radical challenges in writing instruction, for rearticulations of disciplinary boundaries' that emerge in this context (Crow & O'Neill,

2002: 8), there is much to consider in terms of the measurable sense of community within independent writing programs. The creative writing discipline is not alone in its adjuvant status in the English department. Despite its intellectual claim to share with the hard sciences, composition studies has long been referred to as a service field, the work-horses of the department. The problems of composition are said to be 'deeply rooted in the traditions of English departments and in the field's history with them' (Crow & O'Neill, 2002: 8). As a result, compositionists have long imagined professional lives separate from an English department as suggested by Maxine Hairston's 1985 CCCC presidential address in which she calls for the field's intellectual independence. Hairston rallies compositionists to 'establish [their] psychological and intellectual independence from literary critics who are at the center of power in most English departments' (qtd. in Crow & O'Neill, 2002: 2).

Creative writing shares with composition studies a communed history of subordination by literary studies along with a shared interest in writing practices and writing theories. This history, in part, attracts the attention of *creative writing studies*. After all, many of creative writing's practices have some foundational basis in early composition pedagogy, and it would be difficult not to become enmeshed in whatever political agendas may surface in untangling from the embattled field from whence both fields derive.

A space such as the one created by Daniel Royer and Roger Gilles (2002: 32–33) within the department of academic, creative and professional writing at Grand Valley State University, might mean 'twice as many writing courses' for creative writing students, a curriculum model approaching 'that of art and design, where studio courses outnumber content courses – but where "content" naturally informs each and every studio course'. For creative writing students it is a space that is not about literature or writing so much as a location for 'theories about writing and the teaching of writing and theories of reading' (p. 33). It means cross-fertilization possibilities such as merges with media studies – team-taught classes by composition specialists, poets, fictionists, technical communication specialists and media scholars. Bridging such a divide has research implications for the ways students think, read, study, learn and write in such an integrated, yet collaborative model.

Although there are interesting and innovative gains for *creative writing studies* in this space constructed as an independent writing program, what becomes lost, coincidentally, relates to the autonomous gains we might experience as an independent academic discipline, and it is this independence that bears more weight than what a united writing community such as the one described here might court. In addition, our 'divorce' from English studies (if the concept of a marriage can be loosely applied to this relational context), may leave us uncertain, wondering if another relationship so soon is not 'simply shacking up with another "oppressor"' (Crow & O'Neill, 2002: 3). There are other space locations such as the creative writing program at the University of North Carolina at Wilmington, which claims not only its own facility but also its own administrative function. Such an enterprise requires an inventory of program components, a finite number of assets and a tailored curriculum. Perhaps free-standing operations function as centers of excellence much in the same way as certain medical centers become known for their areas of expertise. There are many advantages here, but some may worry that defining a program niche (a specialization) carves out the teaching of certain courses and means resisting extended opportunities that may limit program growth. It works well for the creative writing program at the University of North Carolina at Wilmington because, according to Philip Gerard, chair of the program, 'it is comfortable in knowing what it does best'.[1]

In imagining how we might profit from aligning with independent writing programs, we might ask what new courses could be developed that would incorporate team-teaching opportunities as well as cross-fertilization with those in the fields of composition, professional writing and technical communications so as to add more depth and relativism to a *creative writing studies* program design?

Creative Writing Studies and Composition Studies

A less circumscribed version of the independent writing program is one that incorporates a number of spatial properties for *creative writing studies* aligned with composition in a number of ways: as an intersection between the two fields, a minor or major program track, a concentration within disciplinary studies or a blending or blurring of discipline lines. Among the first to suggest a natural relationship between creative writing and composition are Moxley and Bishop. In 'Tearing down the walls: Engaging the imagination', Moxley (1989: 25) writes that 'engaging students' imaginations', a process he sees as the primary purpose of our instruction, 'requires an interdisciplinary approach, one which brings together creative writing, literature, criticism, and composition'. In 'Crossing the lines: On creative composition and composing creative writing', Bishop (1994: 181) asserts that '[w]e need to be crossing the line between composition and creative writing far more often than we do'. Marie Ponset and Rosemary Deen agree that there is 'no essential difference between writing a poem and writing an essay' (qtd. in Bishop, 1994: 190).

If we believe as Ponset and Deen do that 'all students of writing are creative, that they are always writing literature, and that writing processes have basic commonalities' (qtd. in Bishop, 1994: 190), then what lessons can each discipline learn from the other? Ostrom (1994: xxi) tells us that there are those who believe '(so-called) imaginative writing has a greater role to play in (so-called) basic and first-year writing'. In addition, Ted Lardner (1999: 72) postures that creative writing has 'important lessons to learn from composition in reference to process, pedagogy, and epistemology'. Whether students are writing a rhetorical analysis for composition class or developing a story or poem for a creative writing course, both processes combine some elements of creating and composing. In addition, 'both are grounded in some degree of reality, and both involve some use of the imagination. Both kinds of writing include the subjectivity of the writer' (Miller, 2005: 43). Each requires planning, drafting and recursive processes and employs 'a reader-response theory [which] persuades that meaning does not reside solely in the text, inserted once and for all by authorial agency' (Bishop, 1994: 191). 'Meaning', as Bishop (1994: 191) contends, 'is constructed by authors in conjunction with a reading and a reader'. She asks us to consider 'that for years we may have been reading a wealth of "imaginative" and "creative" essays even when we have assigned them and evaluated them as non-fiction work' (1994: 192). In addition, Bishop claims that 'it is also possible then to visualize the infinity of shaped "family stories" and "true experiences" that comprise the beginning composition of generations of creative writing students' (1994: 192). An intersection between composition and *creative writing studies* seems reasonable to me; however, as Bishop contends, 'the old, limiting distinctions ... were given primacy because they helped keep our selves and our academic territories well and safely sorted' (1994: 192). These 'limiting distinctions' continue to be major stumbling blocks to the intersection of composition and *creative writing studies*.

Although creative writing and composition were considered one and the same in the early years of Harvard English education, their bifurcated tracts since then are one indication why their intersection remains incomplete today. To begin, the protraction of their degree-tracks differ. Creative writing, once perceived as an arts studio degree, developed MFA programs while compositionists formed PhD studies in rhetoric. Consequently, Vandenberg (2004: 8) reports, '[a]s creative writing was defining itself against the research ethos, rhetoric and composition, following literary studies, was buying into it'. Compositionists became significantly focused on writing processes and pedagogical approaches and expressed some relative interest in creative writing. Moxley, for example, published *Creative*

Writing in America (1989), which is said to be 'the seminal work about creative writing informed by composition pedagogy' (Vandenberg, 2004: 9). Bishop responds to how Moxley's composition pedagogy might inform creative writing. She suggests:

> ... that knowledge in that field will redefine our understanding of creativity as 'the natural consequence of learning, involvement, and commitment'. Moxley discusses language studies and composing research; he looks at the scientific method, hemispheric brain research, and writing productivity. In doing so, he claims that it is possible to develop theories of teaching creative writing, and he begins to map out the resources for developing a theory-based pedagogy. (1992b: 426)

After the release of *Creative Writing in America* in 1989, Haake recalls her anticipation that NCTE, the publisher of Moxley's collection, would roll out a whole series of texts on creative writing pedagogies. This production did not transpire, but if it had one wonders if such attention to pedagogy and practice might have stimulated more interest in such an intersection; certainly, such a study would have advanced the emergence of *creative writing studies*. Moxley's book was followed by *Colors of a Different Horse* (1994), edited by Bishop and Ostrom, and once again, contributions, in particular Ostrom's introduction and a section on 'Rethinking, (re)vision, and collaboration', attempted, in part, to consider the intersection between creative writing and composition.

Vandenberg adds to the list of the above pedagogues interested in the topic of overlapping the interstitial spaces between composition and *creative writing studies* by including David Starkey's (1998) perspective in *Teaching Writing Creatively*. Starkey endorses what he calls a 'polyculturalist' approach to writing instruction constructed by 'teacher theorists who, over the years, have actively cross-pollinated areas of writing that had once been isolated from each other' (qtd. in Vandenberg, 2004: 9). Then there is Mayers (2005), poet and compositionist, who makes a plausible case in *(Re)Writing Craft: Composition, Creative Writing, and the Future of English Studies* for a hybridized field of inquiry which joins composition and creative writing as 'writing studies' (p. 114). One of the mitigating factors behind such a conjoining is a need to offset 'literary studies as the rightful center of English studies' (Mayers, 2005: 133). Mayers proposes that this shift in infrastructure is possible through 'a concerted effort to alter one of the fundamental dynamics of the disciplines at large' (2005: 133). At the very least, he notes, 'compositionists and creative writers will have to put aside their very significant professional differences long enough to realize that working together ... they can accomplish more than they can by working separately' (2005: 133). Mayers maps out the necessary groundwork for such a structural change which requires, among many other adjustments, converging composition and creative writing practices within three of the core undergraduate courses: first-year composition, introduction to creative writing and the writing about literature course.

Vandenberg (2004: 9) informs us that '[a] clear sign of a field's maturation and stability is the move to claim influence for one's own scholarship discourse on that of another field'. Most of the movement towards an intersection or union between the discipline of creative writing (or *creative writing studies*) and composition studies has been executed by compositionists or those *writer-teachers* who find it difficult to shift their personas when they enter their creative writing and composition classrooms. Add to the mix, the increasingly generous space in journals like *College Composition and Communication* (CCC) and *College English* (which devoted an entire issue to creative writing in 2003) to essays on creative writing pedagogy and/or reflections of the field's composition influence. Combine this direction with the rise of creative writing sessions at the *College Composition and Communication* Conventions since 1996, and it becomes apparent that 'composition has claimed creative writing as a correlative' (Vandenburg, 2004: 10) despite the dismissal of creative writing's value by some compositionists who bemoan the research differences between composition and creative writing along with the isolationist posture of creative writing. Some complain that creative writing offers limited defined transdisciplinary service across the curriculum, or as Kimberly Andrews admits, '[s]ome of us dismiss creative writing for pedagogies seen as habitual, narrow, and uninterrogated (and some creative writing teachers share that critique), or for absent research, or for perspectives and preoccupations that seem naïve in (1) a world of writers with practical needs or (2) a world whose discursive practices sorely need critique' (qtd. in Hesse, 2011: 33). For those who see creative writing as a corollary to composition studies, it remains questionable, if creative writers are attentive to composition's dialogue about creative writing, and if they are listening, there is no real movement to suggest their interest in such a space. In fact, there is interesting channeling by creative writing away from composition and toward more integration within the university's general education curriculum. With the backdrop of what creative writing can offer the creative industries in today's current market, Steve Healey offers a more radical approach to the relationship between composition and creative writing, suggesting that 'creative writing could eventually take the place of composition as the primary practical service course of English departments across the country –

not simply', he says, 'because students want to write poems and stories, but because they are hungry for creative skills and because creative skills are becoming more valuable in the workplace than the rigid thesis-driving thinking of traditional composition.'[2]

As someone whose feet are in both fields, I endorse the blurring of lines between *creative writing studies* and composition studies. And to that point, it is difficult *not* to consider overlapping properties given the functional interdisciplinary of more and more teachers today. In my own case, my higher education includes creative writing and rhetoric and composition, my writing practices include fiction and scholarly publications and presentations, my teaching pedagogy is informed by both disciplines, and my research methods mix observation and experiential skills with inquiry and pedagogical scholarship. As one of many practitioners who shares creative writing and composition practices in her pedagogical approaches, I represent a fused model of a collective identity, one that influences my students, my colleagues and my field to the degree that I can, but the shifts in structural models that Mayers argues for, such determinant programmatic directions and praxes are beyond the capabilities of such an intersection. A merger remains abstract because the fields stay entrenched in their own histories, conferences, professional organizations, practices and program development.

Creative writers, for the most part, are suspicious of composition's theoretical advances. Ritter (2001), also a writer and teacher of creative writing and composition, points to the structure of graduate degrees offered to its creative writing students as one reason for this withdrawal. She asserts that both MFA and PhD programs in creative writing 'by design encourage writers to become islands adrift professionally and intellectually from their larger English departments' (p. 209). As a field, many creative writing teachers are resistant to a discourse that includes theory and pedagogy, and Ritter suggests the lack of training in these areas explains why creative writers are less interested in the research of ways in which creative writers read, write and teach. AWP compounds this problem when it disregards an endorsement of graduate training in the preparation of teaching. If we are products of our training as Judith Harris suggests when she notes, '[i]n prioritizing the writing skills that will best prove students' proficiency, teachers tend to perpetuate biases that are embedded in their own training and predilections', then it is no wonder that creative writers take on, what Ritter refers to as 'collective academic identities'. In the field of creative writing, we see ourselves as 'writers' and 'artists' *as opposed to* 'teachers' or 'scholars' (p. 210).

The distinction between our conferences reinforces this perception. Douglas Hesse (2011: 32) points to the 'tellingly metonymic of contrasts between academic creative writing and composition studies' present in the audience each conference targets. 'CCCC features writing teachers who are also scholars of rhetoric, writing, and communication', he notes, while 'AWP features writers who are often teachers and, very occasionally, scholars of writing' (p. 32) – although as a sidebar, AWP has already increased the number of its 2012 pedagogy forums based on the current interest in these sessions, so perhaps the tides are shifting some. Moreover, composition's teaching training versus creative writing's lack of such training would ultimately leave such a space conflicted over how student writers might be taught.

The academic home provided for *creative writing studies* by composition studies is one in which creative writers remain suspect. I return to Moxley (1989), who makes two excellent points: first, that 'the general segregation of creative writing from literature and composition corrodes the development of a literacy culture', and second, that 'our passion for specialization within writing departments has caused us to divide and subdivide (potentially) consolidating processes of discovering and shaping meaning' (1989: 25). Foucault's concept of space seems reasonable here, for as he relates space, knowledge and power as that which is necessarily related, he notes 'it is somewhat arbitrary to try to dissociate the effective practice of freedom by people, the practice of social relations, and the spatial distributions in which they find themselves. If they are separated, they become impossible to understand' (qtd. in Crampton & Elden, 2007: 9).

Perhaps the current 'spatial distributions' of *creative writing studies* and composition have bearing on our inability to intersect and this 'separation of sorts' impedes our understanding of one another. Feasibly, 'spatiality occurs as an integral part of a larger concern – as a tool analysis rather than merely an object of it' (qtd. in Crampton & Elden, 2007: 9), and if that is the case, then there is work for creative writing to do in its field, in redefining its space, power, knowledge. One area that might bring the disciplines closer is that of digital media writing. Renowned composition scholar and teacher Andrea Lunsford reminds us that '[w]e're in the midst of a literacy revolution the likes of which we haven't seen since Greek civilization' (qtd. in Thompson, 2009). Her latest studies indicate that such public spaces as 'Twitter , Facebook , and other social writing spaces are helping [students] learn to make savvy and rhetorically appropriate choices in their writing' (qtd. in Thompson, 2009). As students engage in digital media, they are 'building ... a writing culture' (Kathleen Yancy qtd. in Hesse, 2011: 45) that envisions, according to a recent article in *Seed* magazine 'nearly everyone publishing by 2013' (qtd. in Hesse, 2011: 45). Creative writing is moving in this compositional direction with programs like Stanford's undergraduate program, which offers new media courses such as 'Storytelling Through Any Means Necessary' (Day et al., 2011) or other university programs that use space theory in interesting ways (hypertext, photos, maps, videos, podcasts, vlogs, blogs, wikis, music) that interface with textual dimensions, digital tangibles and online platforms. 'Fiction is already hyperlife', one graduate student presenting on a 2011 AWP panel commented, 'so hypertext is one step further.'[3] It seems reasonable that such interfaces will propel *creative writing studies* into new and interesting spaces. For the time being though, until *creative writing studies* can become even more situated as a research field and as an academic curricular entity, the segregation and division that Moxley refers to remain as a mostly theoretical binary between *creative writing studies* and composition.

The Academic Home for *Creative Writing Studies*

It is in this space, the space Foucault reserves as a space of freedom that I argue for the academic home of *creative writing studies*. Defined by Mayers (2009: 218) in a special panel 2008 MLA presentation and in a recent *College English* article, *creative writing studies* is 'a still-emerging enterprise that has been set in motion by some of the problems and internal contradictions of creative writing', and as such, it 'is a field of scholarly inquiry and research'. As a scholarly field of inquiry and research though, *creative writing studies* is not a new *concept*; in fact, Bishop can be said to have pioneered its beginnings with her spatialization of creative writing and composition as an intersection. Our creative writing colleagues across the ocean – the United Kingdom and Australia, in particular – have partnered with criticism, research and scholarship from the start of their program development as they were unencumbered by the history that confines the United States' discipline. The difference between these university creative writing programs and those in the United States is that '[t]here is no long standing tradition in Creative Writing in these countries which needed to be "reformed", and no perceived contribution to an impoverished or standardization of literary culture' (Dawson, 2007: 83). Both the UK and Australia have 'developed [their] disciplinary identity through an engagement with Theory, rather than changing in response to it' (Dawson, 2007: 83). But the United States is moving in interesting multifaceted directions, redefining not only its space but its design and its options for growth in so many areas.

I return then to Foucault's concept of space as a space of freedom, as unconstrained by barriers. Foucault adds, '[s]uch is the power of language: that which is woven of space elicits space, gives itself space through an originary opening and removes space to take it back into language' (qtd.

in Crampton & Elden, 2007: 7) – such language exists in the academic home of *creative writing studies* – in the power, the knowledge and the space of *creative writing studies*. This academic home situates the practitioners and scholars of *creative writing studies* shoulder-to-shoulder with colleagues in composition studies and literary studies, encourages its mobility across university campuses in its merging with creative arts, business and communications disciplines, and extends its reach beyond the academy to explore creative industry opportunities, internships, community outreach and literary citizenship. I have argued for the establishment of *creative writing studies*, outlined the steps to advance its emergence and suggested that its conceptual space is more critical than its physical space. The space that *creative writing studies* occupies must be that which allows *creative writing studies* to become pedagogically and programmatically sound, as well as productive and meaningful to the academy, its profession, its creative economy, and, critically, to its student body. As a discipline, it must continue its necessary field of inquiry, scholarship, and research as well as advocate for its own identity at the public and institutional level.

Notes

1. I had an opportunity to chat with Philip Gerard at the 2011 AWP conference about the creative writing program facility at the University of North Carolina at Wilmington.
2. This comment results from a 12/15/10 email communication with Steve Healey and his contribution to *Key Issues in Creative Writing* 2012c.
3. This was a comment made by a graduate student presenter (currently taking a fiction web-based platform course) at the 2011 AWP session titled 'Creative Online', a session whose description in the AWP program reads: 'What possibilities lie in the malleability of the internet and its multidirectional readability? As the future of fiction becomes increasingly influenced by blogs, social networking and multimedia, writers seek to merge questions of craft with the technological demands of web-based platforms and their potential for instant feedback and editing' (see http://www.awpwriter.org/conference/2010ConfArchive/2010schedThurs.php).

Conclusion: The Legitimacy of *Creative Writing Studies*

My overarching goal in this study is to provide academic legitimacy to the discipline of *creative writing studies*. To best accomplish this objective it is important to explore the discipline's history; more specifically, to understand how the grounding of creative writing's practice informs not only its pedagogies and the theories which underpin its practices, but also its isolation from the central curriculum and its binary opposition with academic critics. With regards to the latter, Ostrom tells us that creative writers often feel underappreciated. They are 'aggrieved', he says, 'always waiting to arrive', and 'even scorned, by those in "literature" and challenged by those in composition and cultural studies' (Ostrom, 1994: xiii). The smallness of creative writers in the scope of the dysfunctional family it calls English studies, Ostrom insists, 'only exacerbates elitism, inbreeding, suspicion, and unproductive conflict' (p. xiii).

Figuratively, along the same lines, it is hard not to connect with Eve Shelnutt's (1989: 11) view of creative writing teachers 'huddled in tight circles reminiscent of Conestoga wagons under attack', and 'as second-class citizens in English departments'. She claims our students come to accept their 'proper place in the intellectual ghettos of English departments', and learn 'they were never meant, heaven forbid, to become creative writers *and* thinkers too' (p. 12, emphasis mine). Scholars criticize the study of creative writing, the classes that convey 'an immoral disregard for great literary monuments', the writing processes which are 'too intuitive and naïve at best', and 'irrational and ignorant at worst' (Fenza, 2000). Creative writing classrooms are 'occasions for self-indulgence, confessional exhibitionism', and 'hardly the stuff for the rigors of an academic discipline' (Fenza, 2000). Those who teach creative writing complain of disparate hiring practices, of perceptions that the area of creative writing is soft and trivial, only a fun activity, anti-intellectual and 'touchy-feely'.

Some of the skepticism between creative writers and those in literary studies are located in the way the discipline is defined, the lore and perception both from within the academy and from the popular images of writing and writers. Even such basic principles as 'whether we write the writing or the writing writes us', are wrangled with issues of ownership, authority and practice (Haake, 2000: 53).

There was a time in the early 20th century when creative writing and literary studies partnered, when poets, in particular, entered the university and joined literary critics in an unlikely partisan group to fight against the scientific study of literature. Poets became critics, defining, in part, the study of literature from a New Critical view. Even Norman Foerster, who designed the Iowa School of letters, intended for creativity and criticism to be allies in his university curriculum for writers. The discipline, however, became less dually-aligned with creative writing and criticism when Paul Engle dropped the academic track at Iowa and focused instead on the studio method, the workshop prototype practiced in classrooms today. Since the sixties, the 'mystique of professionalism' has given rise to creative writing teachers disregarding the discipline of criticism to become, according to Myers' charge, 'a national staff of writers who teach writers who go on to teach, and to hope for tenure and promotion' (qtd. in Lim, 2003: 163). This sustains, Lim reports, 'the debilitating segregation of writing from criticism and scholarship, of technique from theory' (p. 163).

The workshop model provides a useful pedagogical example of a practice in which the separation of writing from criticism and technique from theory is apparent. As discussed, the century-old workshop has been 'basically unrevised' because there has not, until recently, been any 'rigorous inquiry', which 'offers testimony to its excellence' (Bizzaro, 2004: 296). As creative writing practitioners add to the theoretical and academic scholarship of *creative writing studies* and explore rigorous inquiries into such pedagogies as the workshop model, they will find, as a result, exciting opportunities to flex the workshop's elasticity and complement and complicate its practice.

With an understanding of creative writing's history, even one as brief as I mention here and throughout my discourse, it is not difficult to trace the path that led to creative writing's isolationist location within English studies, nor is it difficult to trace the evolution of some of the interdepartmental disputes and note where and when creative writing as a discipline partnered with criticism and where it separated from the practice of criticism. What is important to also address in the discipline's history is the self-marginalization by some creative writing teachers who resist inquiry and research into their pedagogies, who retreat from theories that underpin their classroom planning and practices, and who replicate the basic workshop model and other methods that idle.

Moreover, self-marginalization in creative writing is also very much connected to 'the absence of teacher training and pedagogical reform in the face of the lore that perpetuates the traditions and customs of the field' (Ritter & Vanderslice, 2007: xiii). This is the lore of the lonely writer in the garret; of long, unbroken passages of inspired writing; of casual classrooms and clustered conversations, of easy 'A's' and cool, eccentric teachers. This is the lore of teaching creative writing, which 'is systemic, pervasive, and rooted in creative writing's isolated academic status, at once frustrating and comforting to the writers and organizations who perpetuate it' (Ritter & Vanderslice, 2007: xiii). One of the more critical ambitions of *creative writing studies* is the training of its graduates in teacher preparation. David Radavich (1999: 110) proposes that 'advanced degrees in creative writing cannot generate the job prospects available even to graduates of more traditional doctoral programs' and that 'there is no profession for which an MFA or PhD in creative writing provides direct training'. There is an urgent need for such training not only to better position creative writing graduates in the marketplace, but as a way to also best prepare instructors who can teach the new skills formulated through the field's inquiries, research and discoveries. This training (and then practice) equates to what amounts to a significant professional paradigm shift as more creative writers welcome inquiries into their field and willingly participate in the scholarship and new identity of their discipline.

As long as there are such vast differences in epistemological studies and pedagogical approaches between the disciplines of English studies, tensions will remain, and faculty will question why and how creative writing is still a tenant in the English department that houses it. However, a discipline such as *creative writing studies* which explores the pedagogy and theory of its field, establishes its own scholarship, identifies its own markers of professional difference, trains its graduates in teacher preparation, develops new courses and venues for passing new skills on to its students, may bridge some of the widened gap that has occurred over the embattled territory of what many consider to be a mostly hegemonic English department. *Creative writing studies* moves beyond its opposition to criticism so as to develop its own scholarship and identity. As an academic discipline, it may not eliminate interdepartmental tensions, but there is hope that because some points of *creative writing studies* overlap with both literary studies and composition studies that the emergent discipline will create more positive movement in redefining the structure of English studies.

Moreover, Mayers (2009) considers the fate of creative writing in a dysfunctional English department. He notes that should there be a split between composition studies and literary studies (for example, composition studies joins an independent writing program), then 'creative writers may be placed in undesirable positions', as they are 'compelled to choose between two imperfect options' (2009: 227). Mayers' scenario is further 'validation for the importance of *creative writing studies* – a field of inquiry that will provide creative writers in academia with the intellectual tools to answer tough questions and face tough choices' (2009: 227).

As an academic discipline in its own right, *creative writing studies* negotiates, accommodates and identifies critical theories. It identifies and negotiates critical theories as it challenges traditional practices as provided in this text through inquiries and research into the workshop model and the discipline's major pedagogical theories. *Creative writing studies* accommodates critical theory as it considers what it draws epistemologically from composition studies and literary studies and then applies, modifies or develops discipline-specific critical writing and reading practices in the creative writing classroom and writing workshop. The vision for practitioners of *creative writing studies* situates the writer and the discipline within a broader theoretical base. Part of the imperative in *creative writing studies* is the constant questioning and challenging of existing practices. We are that much closer to accepting *creative writing studies* than we were a decade ago. As the discipline aims for a more diversified body of knowledge, it also rethinks its signature pedagogy, dominant teaching strategies and its perspectives on theory and scholarship. It becomes more expansive, flexible, collaborative, enriched and independent. As *creative writing studies* becomes better situated as a research field and as an academic curricular entity, it will soon receive the attention it deserves. As it does, *creative writing studies* will add more meaning to the academy, its profession and its diverse student body.

References

Abrams, M.H. (1953) *The Mirror and the Lamp*. London: Oxford UP.
Adams, K.H. (1993) *A History of Professional Writing Instruction in American Colleges*. Dallas: So. Methodist UP.
Aldridge, J. (1990) The new assembly-line fiction. *American Scholar* 59, 17–38.
Anderson, L. (1991) Using reader-response theory in the introductory literature classroom. *College Literature* 18 (2) (Jun.), 41–145.
AWP (2010) Guide to writing programs. Online at http://guide.awpwriter.org/
Barr, J. (2006) American poetry in the new century. *Poetry* 188 (5), 433–441.
Behns, R. (1992) *The Practice of Poetry: Writing Exercises from Poets Who Teach*. New York: Harper.
Berlin, J.E. (1982) Contemporary composition: The major pedagogical theories. *College English* 44 (80) (Dec.), 765–777.
Berlin, J.E. (1987a) *Rhetoric and Reality*. Carbondale: So. Illinois UP.
Berlin, J.E. (1987b) *Writing Instruction in American Colleges, 1900–1985*. Carbondale: So. Illinois UP.
Bernays, A. and Painter, P. (1995) *What If? Writing Exercises for Fiction Writers*. New York: Harper.
Bishop, W. (1990) *Released Into Language: Options for Teaching Creative Writing*. Urbana: NCTE.
Bishop, W. (1992a) On being in the same boat. *AWP Chronicle* (March/April) http://elink.awpwriter.org/m/awpChron/articles/wbishop01.lasso. Accessed 23 October 2010.
Bishop, W. (1992b) Rev. of *Creative Writing in America*. *JAC* 10: 2 http://www.jacweb.org/Archived_volumes/Text_articles/V10_I2_Rev_Bishop.htm. Accessed 09 August 2010.
Bishop, W. (1994) Crossing the lines: On creative composition and composing creative Writing. In W. Bishop and H. Ostrom (eds) *Colors of a Different Horse: Rethinking Creative Writing Theory and Pedagogy* (pp. 181–197). Urbana: NCTE.
Bishop, W. and Ostrom, H. (eds) (1994) *Colors of a Different Horse*. Urbana: NCTE.
Bishop, W. and Starkey, D. (2006) *Keywords in Creative Writing*. Logan: Utah State UP.
Bizzaro, P. (1993) *Responding to Student Poems*. Urbana: NCTE.
Bizzaro, P. (1994) Reading the creative writing course: The teachers' many selves, in W. Bishop and H. Ostrom (eds) *Colors of a Different Horse* (pp. 234–247). Urbana: NCTE.
Bizzaro, P. (1998) Should I write the essay or finish a poem? Teaching writing creatively. *CCC* 49 (2), 285–297.

Bizzaro, P. (2004) Research and reflections: The special case of creative writing. *College English* 66 (3) (Jan), 294–309.
Bizzaro, P. and McClanahan, M. (2007) Putting wings on the invisible: Voice, authorship and the authentic self. In K. Ritter and S. Vanderlice (eds) *Can it Really be Taught?* (77–90). Portsmouth: Boynton/Cook.
Bizzell, P. (1982) Cognition, convention, and certainty: What we need to know about writing. *Journal of Rhetorical History* 3, 213–243.
Bly, C. (2001) *Beyond the Writers' Workshop*. New York: Anchor Books.
Blythe, H. and Sweet, C. (2008) The new writing community: A new model for the creative writing Classroom. *Pedagogy* 8 (2), 305–325.
Boden, M.A. (2004) *The Creative Mind: Myths and Mechanisms*. London: Routledge.
Bontley, T. (2007) Creative writing in the academy. *Sewanee Review* 115 (1) (Winter), iii–v.
Bracher, M. (1999) *The Writer Cure*. Carbondale: Southern Illinois UP.
Brooke, R. (1987) Lacan, transference, and writing instruction. *College English* 49 (6), 679–691.
Brooks, C. (1979) *Modern Poetry and the Tradition*, reprint. North Carolina: University of North Carolina Press.
Brooks, C. and Warren, R.P. (1938) *Understanding Poetry*. New York: Henry Holt.
Brooks, C. and Warren, R.P. (1979) *Understanding Fiction*, 3rd edition. New Jersey: Prentice Hall Publishing.
Brophy, K. (2000) Taming the contemporary. *TEXT* 4 (1) (April) <http://www.textjournal.com.au/april00/brophy.htm>. Accessed 12 September 2010.
Bruffee, K.A. (1984) Collaborative learning and the 'Conversation of Mankind'. *College English* 46 (7) (Nov.), 635–652.
Bruns, A. and Brien, D.L. (n.d.) Teaching electronic creative writing: A report from the creative industries frontline. <http://snurb.info/files/31-03-03%20Teaching%20Electronic%20Creative%20Writing.pdf>. Accessed 12 August 2011.
Budman, R. (n.d.) From where you dream: An interview with Robert Olen Butler', *Del Sol Literary Dialogues*. http://webdelsol.com/Literary_Dialogues/interview-wds-butler.htm. Accessed 20 May 2010.
Burriesci, M. (2008) NEA report shows that steep decline in American reading skills will have significant long-term negative effects on society. AWP *Writer's Chronicle* 40 (40) (Feb.), 1–2. http://www.awpwriter.org/pdf/mburriesci01.pdf. Accessed 16 October 2010.
Burroway, J. (2010) *Imaginative Writing: The Elements of Craft*, 3rd edition. New York: Longman.
Cain, M.A. (2010) 'A Space of Radical Openness': Re-Visioning the Creative Writing Workshop. In D. Donnelly (ed.) *Does the Writing Workshop Still Work?* (pp. 216–229). Bristol: Multilingual Matters.
Cain, W.E. (1982) The institutionalization of the New Criticism. *MLN*, Comparative Literature 97 (5) (Dec.), 1101–1120.
Cain, W.E. (1984) *The Crisis in Criticism*. Baltimore: John Hopkins UP.
Candy, L. (2006) Practice-based research: A guide, creativity and cognition studios. University of Technology <http://www.creativityandcognition.com>. Accessed 13 January 2011.

Cantrell, M. (2005) Teaching and evaluation: Why bother? In A. Leahy (ed.) *Power and Identity in the Creative Writing Classroom* (pp. 65–76). Clevedon: Multilingual Matters.
Carey, J., Webb, J. and Brien, D.L. (2008) A plethora of policies: Examining creative research higher degrees in Australia. *The Creativity and Uncertainty Papers*, AAWP. <http://www.aawp.org.au/files/CareyWebbBrien.pdf>. Accessed 18 February 2011.
Carlson, S. (2005) The new generation goes to college. *The Chronicle of Higher Education*. (Oct.) <http://chronicle.com/free/v52/i07/07a03401.htm?> Accessed 02 March 2010.
Carr, N. (2008) Is Google making us stupid? *Atlantic* (Jul./Aug.) <http://www.theatlantic.com/doc/200807/google>. Accessed 02 March 2010.
Ciabattari, J. (2005) Workshop: A revolution of sensibility. *Poets & Writers* (Jan/Feb) <http://www.pw.org>. Accessed 14 April 2010.
Ciardi, J. (1959) *How Does a Poem Mean?* Cambridge: The Riverside Press.
Clark, K. (1999) Study as practice: On creative writing & the English curriculum. *Writer's Chronicle* (Sept.) <http://elink.awpwriter.org/m/awpChron/articles/kclark01.lasso>. Accessed 19 April 2010.
Clark, M. H. (2003) Touched by an angel. *The Washington Post Book World*.
Clausen, C. (1997) Reading closely again. *Commentary* 103 (2) (Feb.), 54–57.
Cole, C. (2007) How the university workshop hinders new writers from engaging with ideas (and what to do about it). *Segue Online Literary Journal*, 1–13. Miami University Middletown <http://www.mid.muohio.edu/segue>. Accessed 12 December 2010.
Cook, J. (2005) Creative writing as a research method. In G. Griffin (ed.) *Research Methods for English Studies* (pp. 195–211). Edinburgh: Edinburgh P.
Cook, P., Melchior, I., Radford, R.F., Adler, C.S., Cohen, S. Knight, W.E. and Abel, R.H. (1989) Creative writers' report: Mastering the craft. In J. Moxley (ed.) *Creative Writing in America* (pp. 247–260). Urbana: NCTE.
Cooley, N. (2003) Literary legacies and critical transformations: Teaching creative writing in the public urban university. *Pedagogy* 3 (1) 99–103.
Crampton, J.W. and Elden, S. (2007) Introduction: Space, knowledge and power: Foucault and geography. In J. Crampton and S. Elden (eds) *Space, Knowledge and Power: Foucault and Geography* (1–16). Williston: Ashgate.
Crow, A. and O'Neill, P. (2002) Introduction: Cautionary tales about change. In P. O'Neill, A. Crow and L.W. Burton (eds) *A Field of Dreams: Independent Writing Programs and the Future of Composition Studies* (pp. 1–18). Logan: Utah State UP.
Davidson, C. and Fraser, G. (2006) Poetry. In G. Harper (ed.) *Teaching Creative Writing* (pp. 21–33). London: Continuum.
Davis, T.F. and Womack, K. (2002) *Formalist Criticism and Reader-Response Theory*. New York: Palgrave.
Dawson, P. (2005) *Creative Writing and the New Humanities*. Oxford: Routledge.
Dawson, P. (2007) The future of creative writing. In S. Earnshaw (ed.) *The Handbook of Creative Writing* (pp. 78–90). Edinburgh: Edinburgh UP.
Day, C., Leahy, A. and Vanderslice, S. (2011) Where are we going next: A conversation about creative writing pedagogy (Pt. 1). *Fiction Writers Review* (Feb.) <http://fictionwritersreview.com/essays/where-are-we-going-next-a-conversation-about-creative-writing-pedagogy-pt-1>. Accessed 4 April 2011.
Delaney, E.J. (2007) Where great writers are made. *The Atlantic* (Fiction Issue) <http://www.theatlantic.com/doc/200708/edward-delaney-mfa>. Accessed 17 January 2010.

Delbanco, N. (2004) *The Sincerest Form: Writing Fiction by Imitation*. New York: McGraw-Hill.
Deletiner, C. (1992) Crossing lines. *College English* 54 (7), 809–817.
Domina, L. (1994) The body of my work is not just a metaphor. In W. Bishop and H. Ostrom (eds) *Colors of a Different Horse* (pp. 27–34). Urbana: NCTE.
Donnelly, D. (ed.) (2010) *Does the Writing Workshop Still Work?* Bristol: Multilingual Matters.
Donnelly, D. (2011) Creative writing and composition: Rewriting the lines. In P. Bizzaro, A. Culhane and D. Cook (eds) *Composing Ourselves as Writer-Teacher-Writers: Starting with Wendy Bishop* (pp. 105–115). New York: Hampton Press, Inc.
Eagleton, T. (1983) *Literary Theory: An Introduction*. Minneapolis: U of Minnesota P.
Earnshaw, S. (2007) The writer as artist. In S. Earnshaw (ed.) *The Handbook of Creative Writing* (pp. 65–77). Edinburgh: Edinburgh UP.
Ede, L. and Lunsford, A. (1984) Audience addressed/audience invoked: The role of audience in composition theory and pedagogy. *College Composition and Communications* 35, 155–173.
Elliot, G. (1994) Pedagogy in penumbra: Teaching, writing, and feminism in the fiction Workshop. In W. Bishop and H. Ostrom (eds) *Colors of a Different Horse* (pp. 100–130). Urbana: NCTE.
Fenza, D.W. (2000) Creative writing & its discontents. *Writer's Chronicle* (March/April) <http://www.awpwriter.org/magazine/writers/fenza01.htm>. Accessed 12 December 2010.
Fish, S. (2005) *Is There a Text in This Class?* Cambridge: Harvard UP.
Foucault, M. (1980) Truth and power. In C. Gordon (ed.) *Power Knowledge: Selected Interviews and Other Writings 1972–1977* (pp. 109–133). New York: Pantheon.
Friedman, T. (2005) *The World is Flat: A Brief History of the Twenty-First Century*. New York: Farrar, Straus and Giroux.
Fulkerson, R. (1990) Composition theory in the eighties: Axiological consensus and paradigmatic diversity. *CCC* 41 (4) (Dec.), 409–429.
Galef, D. (2000) Words, words, words. In P.C. Herman (ed.) *Day Late, Dollar Short* (pp. 161–174). Albany: SUNY P.
Garber, E. and Ramjerdi, J. (1994) Reflections on the teaching of creative writing: A correspondence. In W. Bishop and H. Ostrom (eds) *Colors of a Different Horse* (pp. 8–26). Urbana: NCTE.
Garrett, G. (1989) The future of creative writing programs. In J. Moxley (ed.) *Creative Writing in America: Theory and Pedagogy* (pp. 47–61). Urbana: NCTE.
Gee, J.P. (2003) *What Video Games Have to Teach Us About Learning and Literacy*. New York: Palgrave.
Gillman, C. P. (2000) The yellow wallpaper. In R.V. Cassill and R. Bausch (eds) *The Norton Anthology of Short Fiction* (6th edn) (pp. 675–687). New York: W.W. Norton & Co.
Gioia, D. (1991) Can poetry matter? *Atlantic Monthly* 276 (May), 94–106.
Graff, G. (1987) *Professing Literature*. Chicago: University of Chicago Press.
Graff, G. (1995) Conflict pedagogy and student experience. *CCC* 46 (2) (May), 276–279.
Green, C. (2001) Materializing the sublime reader: Cultural studies, reader response, and community service in the creative writing workshop. *College English* 64 (2) (Nov.), 153–174.

Grimes, T. (1999) Workshop and the writing life. In T. Grimes (ed.) *The Workshop: Seven Decades of the Iowa Writers' Workshop* (pp. 1–15). New York: Hyperion.
Gross, P. (2010) Small worlds: What works in workshops if and when they do? In D. Donnelly (ed.) *Does the Writing Workshop Still Work?* (pp. 52–62). Bristol: Multilingual Matters.
Gudding, G. (1999) From Petit to Langpo: A history of solipsism and experience in mainstream poetics since the rise of creative writing. *Flash Point Magazine* (Summer 3) <http://www.Flashpointmag.com/guddin_1.htm>. Accessed 11 October 2010.
Guevara, M.K. (1998) Out of the ashtray: Revivifying creative writing classes. *AWP* (Mar./Apr.) <http://elink.awpwriter.org/m/awpChron/articles/mguevara01.lasso. Accessed 09 October 2010>.
Haake, K. (1994) Teaching creative writing if the shoe fits. In W. Bishop and H. Ostrom (eds) *Color of a Different Horse* (77–99). Urbana: NCTE.
Haake, K. (2000) *What Our Speech Disrupts: Feminism and Creative Writing Studies*. Urbana: NCTE.
Haake, K. (2005) Dismantling authority: Teaching what we do not know. In A. Leahy (ed.) *Power and Identity in the Creative Writing Classroom* (pp. 98–105). Clevedon: Multilingual Matters.
Haake, K. (2007) Against reading. In K. Ritter and S. Vanderslice (eds) *Can it Really be Taught?* (pp. 14–27). Portsmouth: Boynton/Cook.
Haake, K. (2010) Re-envisioning the workshop: Hybrid classrooms, hybrid texts. In D. Donnelly (ed.) *Does the Writing Workshop Still Work?* (pp. 182–193). Bristol: Multilingual Matters.
Hall, D. (1998) Poetry and ambition. *The Kenyon Review* (new series) 5 (4), 90–104.
Harper, G. (2006) Introduction. In G. Harper (ed.) *Teaching Creative Writing* (pp. 1–7). London: Continuum.
Harper, G. (2008) Creative writing: Words as practice-led research. *Journal of Visual Arts Practice* 7 (2), 161–171.
Harper, G. (2010) Foreword: On Experience. In D. Donnelly (ed.) *Does the Writing Workshop Still Work?* (xv–xx). Bristol: Multilingual Matters.
Harris, J. (2001) Re-writing the subject: Psychoanalytic approaches to creative writing and composition pedagogy. *College English* 64 (2), 175–204.
Healey, S. (2009) The rise of creative writing & the new value of creativity. *The Writers Chronicle* 41 (4) 30–39.
Hecq, D. and Banagan, R. (2010) Practice, research, and their phantom limb. *TEXT* 14 (1) <http://www.textjournal.com.au/april10/hecq_banagan_rev.htm>. Accessed 02 November 2010.
Hempel, A. (1983) In the cemetery where Al Jolson is buried. In R. Bausch and R.V. Cassill (eds) *The Norton Anthology of Short Fiction* (7th edn) (pp. 666–672). New York: W.W. Norton & Co.
Hesse, D. (2011) The place of creative writing in composition studies. *College Composition and Communication* 62 (1) (Sept), 31–52.
Howarth, P. (2007) Creative writing and Schiller's aesthetic education. *Journal of Aesthetic Education* 41 (3) (Fall), 41–58.
Hugo, R. (1979) *The Triggering Town: Lectures and Essays on Poetry and Writing*. NY: Norton.

Irvine, C. (2010) 'It's fine, I guess': Problems with the workshop model in college composition Courses. In D. Donnelly (ed.) *Does the Writing Workshop Still Work?* (pp. 130–145). Bristol: Multilingual Matters.
Iser, W. (1974) *The Implied Reader: Patterns of Communication in Prose Fiction from Banyan to Beckett*. Baltimore: Johns Hopkins UP.
Iser, W. (1978) *The Act of Reading*. Baltimore: Johns Hopkins UP.
Iser, W. (1980) The reading process: A phenomenological approach. In J. Thompkins (ed.) *Reader-Response Criticism: From Formalism to Post-Structuralism* (pp. 50–69). Baltimore: Johns Hopkins UP.
Krauth, N. (2000) Where is writing now? Australian University Creative Writing Programs at the end of the millennium. TEXT 4 (1) <http://www.textjournal.com.au/april00/krauth.htm>. Accessed 01 February 2010.
Kroll, J. (2004) The exegesis and the gentle reader/writer. *TEXT Special Issue* 3 <http://www.textjournal.com.au/speciss/issue3/kroll.htm>. Accessed 07 December 2010.
Kroll, J. (2008) Creative practice and/as/is/or research: An overview. In L. Neve and D. Brien (eds) *The Creativity and Uncertainty Papers: The Refereed Proceedings of the 13th Conference of the Australian Association of Writing Programs*, 1–13 <http://aawp.org.au/creativity-and-uncertainty-papers>. Accessed 13 December 2010.
Kroll, J. (2009) The supervisor as practice-led coach and trainer: Getting creative writing doctoral candidates across the finish line. In D. Brien and R. Williamshon (eds) *Special Issue: Supervising the Creative Arts Research Higher Degree: Towards Best Practice* 6, 1–20 <http://www.aawp.org.au/files/Kroll.pdf>. Accessed 13 December 2010.
Kuhl, N. (2005) Personal therapeutic writing vs. literary writing. In A. Leahy (ed.) *Power and Identity in the Creative Writing Classroom* (pp. 3–12). Clevedon: Multilingual Matters.
Lacan, J. (1966) *Ecrits*. Paris: Editions du Seuil.
Lardner, T. (1999) Locating the boundaries of composition and creative writing. CCC 51 (1), 72–77.
Leahy, A. (2005) (ed.) *Power and Identity in the Creative Writing Classroom: The Authority Project*. Clevedon: Multilingual Matters.
Leahy, A. (2007) Creativity, caring, and the easy 'A': Rethinking the role of self-esteem in creative writing pedagogy. In K. Ritter and S. Vanderslice (eds) *Can it Really be Taught?* (pp. 55–66). Portsmouth: Boynton/Cook.
Leahy, A. (2010) Teaching as a creative act: Why the workshop works in creative writing. In D. Donnelly (ed.) *Does the Writing Workshop Still Work?* (pp. 63–77). Bristol: Multilingual Matters.
Levine, G. (1993) The real trouble. *Profession*, 43–45.
Light, G. (1999) Conceiving creative writing in higher education. NAWE <http://www.nawe.co.uk/archive>. Accessed 11 November 2010.
Lim, S. G-l. (2003) The strangeness of creative writing: An institutional query. *Pedagogy* 3, 151–169.
Lynn, S. (1990) A passage into critical theory. *College English* 15 (3), 258–267.
Manolis, A. (2005) Writing the community: Service learning in creative writing. In A. Leahy (ed.) *Power and Identity in the Creative Writing Classroom: The Authority Project* (pp. 141–151). Clevedon: Multilingual Matters.
Mayers, T. (2005) *(Re)Writing Craft*. Pittsburgh: University of Pittsburgh Press.

Mayers, T. (2007) Figuring the future. In K. Ritter and S. Vanderslice (eds) *Can it Really be Taught?* (1–13). Portsmouth: Boynton/Cook.
Mayers, T. (2009) One simple word: From creative writing to creative writing studies. *College English* 71 (3) (Jan.), 217–228.
Mayers, T. (2010) Poetry, f(r)iction, drama: The complex dynamics of audience in the writing Workshop. In D. Donnelly (ed.) *Does the Writing Workshop Still Work?* (pp. 94–104). Bristol: Multilingual Matters.
McGurl, M. (2007) Understanding Iowa: Flannery O'Connor, B.A., M.F.A. *American Literary History* 19 (2), 527–545.
Mearns, H. (1935) *Creative Power*. Garden City: Doubleday.
Meehan, M. (2010) Researcher of the month (April). *Research in the Faculty of Arts and Education* Deacon University Australia <http://www.deakin.edu.au/arts-ed/research/profile/mmeehan.php>. Accessed 11 December 2010.
Menand, L. (2009) Show or tell: Should creative writing be taught? *The New Yorker* (June 8) <http://www.newyorker.com/arts/critics/atlarge/2009/06/08/090608crat atlarge_menand>. Accessed 13 November 2010.
Miller, E.Y. (2005) Reinventing writing classrooms: The combination of creating and Composing. In A. Leahy (ed.) *Power and Identity in the Creative Writing Classroom: The Authority Project* (pp. 39–48). Clevedon: Multilingual Matters.
Minock, M. (1995) Toward a postmodern pedagogy of imitation. *JAC* 15 (3) <http://www.jacweb.org/Archived_volumes/Text_articles/V15_I3_Minock.htm>. Accessed 19 September 2010.
Minot, S. (1976) Creative writing: Start with the student's motive. *CCC* 27 (4) (Dec.), 392–394.
Moxley, J. (1989) Tearing down the walls: Engaging the imagination. In J. Moxley (ed.) *Creative Writing in America: Theory and Pedagogy* (pp. 25–45). Urbana: NCTE.
Moxley, J. (2010) Afterword: Disciplinarity and the future of creative writing studies. In D. Donnelly (ed.) *Does the Writing Workshop Still Work?* (pp. 230–238). Bristol: Multilingual Matters.
Mueke, S. (2010) Public thinking, public feeling: Research tools for creative writing. *TEXT* 14 (1) <http://www.textjournal.com.au/april10/muecke.htm>. Accessed 6 January 2011.
Murphy, A. (1989) Transference and resistance in the basic writing classroom: Problematics and praxis. *CCC* 40 (2) 175–187.
Murray, D. (1989) Unlearning to write. In J. Moxley (ed.) *Creative Writing in America* (pp. 103–113). Urbana: NCTE.
Myers, D.D. (1994) The lessons of creative writing's history. *AWP Chronicle* 26 (1) (Feb) <http://www.awpwriter.org/login/m/awpChron/articles/dgmyers01.lasso>. Accessed 10 August 2010.
Myers, D.G. (1996) *The Elephants Teach: Creative Writing Since 1880*. Chicago: University of Chicago Press.
NAWE (2008) 'Creative Writing Subject Benchmark Statement: Creative Writing Research Benchmark Statement', National Association of Writers in Education (NAWE), assessed 4 January 2010. http://www.nawe.co.uk/writing-in-education/writing-at-university/research.html

North, S. (1987) *The Making of Knowledge in Composition*. Upper Montclair, NJ: Boynton/Cook.
O'Brien, T. (2007) The things they carried. In R. Bausch and R.V. Cassill (eds) *The Norton Anthology of Short Fiction* (7th edn) (pp. 1188–1200). New York: W.W. Norton & Co.
O'Dair, S. (2000) Stars, tenure, and the death of ambition. In P.C. Herman (ed.) *Day Late, Dollar Short* (pp. 45–61). Albany: SUNY P.
Ong, W.J. (1975) The writer's audience is always a fiction. *PMLA* 90, 9–21.
Ostrom, H. (1994) Introduction: Of radishes and shadows, theory and pedagogy. In W. Bishop and H. Ostrom (eds) *Colors of a Different Horse* (xi-xxiii). Urbana: NCTE.
Park, D.B. (1982) The meaning of audience. *College English* 44 (3), 247–257.
Perloff, M. (2006) 'Creative Writing' among the disciplines. *MLA Newsletter* (President's Column) 38 (1) (Spring), 3–4.
Perry, G. (2008) The non-verbal and the verbal: Expanding awareness of practice-led research in creative writing. In L. Neve and D. Brien (eds) *The Creativity and Uncertainty Papers: The Refereed Proceedings of the 13th Conference of the Australian Association of Writing Programs*, AAWP, 1–11 <http://www.aawp.org.au/files/Perry_2008.pdf>. Accessed 10 December 2010.
Perry, G. (2010) Potentially dangerous: Vulnerabilities and risks in the writing workshop. In D. Donnelly (ed.) *Does the Writing Workshop Still Work?* (pp. 117–129). Bristol: Multilingual Matters.
Pink, D. (2004) The MFA is the new MBA. *Harvard Business Review* 82 (2) (Feb), 21–22.
Polkinghorne, D. (1988) *Narrative Knowing and the Human Sciences*. New York: State U of NY P.
Pollack, E. (2007) Flannery O'Connor and the new criticism: A response to Mark McGurl. *American Literary History* 19 (2) (Summer), 546–556.
Porter, J.E. and Sullivan, P.A. (1993) Remapping curricular geography. *Journal of Business and Technical Communication*, 389–422 <http:jbt.sagepub.com/cgi/content/refs/7/4/389>. Accessed 09 August 2010.
Pratt, M.L. (2009) Arts of the contact zone. In D. Bartholomae and A. Petrosky (eds) *Ways of Reading* (5th edn) <http://www.nwe.ufl.edu/~stripp/2504/pratt.html>. Accessed 16 November 2010.
Prose, F. (2006) *Reading Like a Writer*. New York: Harper Collins Publishers.
Radavich, D. (1999) Creative writing in the academy. *Profession*, 110–112.
Ransom, J.C. (1979) *New Criticism* (reprint). Westport: Greenwood Press.
Reilly, L. (2002) An alternative model of 'knowledge' for the arts. *Working Papers in Art and Design* 2 <http://sitem.herts.ac.uk/artdes_research/papers/wpades/vol2/reillyfull.html>. Accessed 06 January 2011.
Revell, D. (2007) *The Art of Attention: A Poet's Eye*. Saint Paul: Graywolf Press.
Ritter, K. (2001) Professional writers/writing professionals: Revamping teacher training in creative writing Ph.D. programs. *College English* 64 (2) (Nov.), 205–227.
Ritter, K. and Vanderslice, S. (2005) Teaching lore: Creative writers and the university. *Profession*, 102–112.
Ritter, K. and Vanderslice, S. (2007) Introduction: Creative writing and the persistence of 'Lore'. In K. Ritter and S. Vanderslice (eds) *Can It Be Taught?* (pp. xi-xx). Portsmouth: Boynton/Cook.

Roe, S. (2010) Introducing masterclasses. In D. Donnelly (ed.) *Does the Writing Workshop Still Work?* (pp. 194–205). Bristol: Multilingual Matters.

Royer, D.J. and Gilles, R. (2002) The origins of a department of academia, creative, and professional writing. In P. O'Neill, A. Crow and L.W. Burton (eds) *A Field of Dreams: Independent Writing Programs and the Future of Composition Studies* (pp. 21–37). Logan: Utah State UP.

Royster, B. (2005) Inspiration, creativity, and crisis: The Romantic myth of the writer meets the contemporary classroom. In A. Leahy (ed.) *Power and Identity in the Creative Writing Classroom: The Authority Project* (pp. 6–38). Clevedon: Multilingual Matters.

Royster, B. (2010) Engaging the individual/social conflict within creative writing pedagogy. In D. Donnelly (ed.) *Does the Writing Workshop Still Work?* (pp. 105–116). Bristol: Multilingual Matters.

Scrivener, S. (2000) Reflection in and on action and practice in creative-production doctoral projects in art and design. *Working Papers in Art and Design* 1 <http://sitem.herts.ac.uk/artdes_research/papers/wpades/vol1/scrivener1.html>. Accessed 4 February 2011.

Shelnutt, E. (1989) Notes from a cell: Creative writing programs in isolation. In J. Moxley (ed.) *Creative Writing in America: Theory and Pedagogy* (pp. 3–24). Urbana: NCTE.

Shulman, L. (2005a) Pedagogies of uncertainty. *Liberal Education* (Spring) <http://www.aacu.org/liberaleducation/le-sp05/le-sp05feature2.cfm>. Accessed 08 August 2010.

Shulman, L. (2005b) Signature pedagogies in the professions. *Daedalus* 134 (3), 52–59.

Siegel, B. (1989) *The American Writer and the University*. Newark: U of Delaware P.

Smith, H. and Dean, R.T. (2009) Introduction: Practice-led research, research-led practice—towards the interactive cyclic web. In H. Smith and R.T. Dean (eds) *Practice-Led Research, Research-Led Practice in the Creative Arts (Research Methods for the Arts and Humanities)* (pp. 1–38). Edinburgh: Edinburgh University Press.

Snodgrass, W.D. (1994) Mentors, fomenters, and tormentors. In R. Dana (ed.) *A Community of Writers: Paul Engle and the Iowa Writers' Workshop* (pp. 119–146). Iowa City: University of Iowa Press.

Sommers, N. (1980) Revision strategies of student writers and experienced writers. *English Language Arts Bulletin* 20 (Winter/Summer), 8–14.

Starkey, D. (1998) *Teaching Writing Creatively*. Portsmouth: Boynton/Cook.

Starkey, D. and Healy, E.K. (2007) 'A better time teaching': A dialogue about pedagogy and the Antioch-LA MFA. In K. Ritter and S. Vanderslice (eds) *Can it Really be Taught?* (pp. 38–45). Portsmouth: Boynton/Cook.

Stoll, E.E. (1932) Literature and life again. *PMLA* 37, 296–297.

Swander, M., Leahy, A. and Cantrell, M. (2007) Theories of creativity and creative writing Pedagogy. In S. Earnshaw (ed.) *The Handbook of Creative Writing* (pp. 11–23). Edinburgh: Edinburgh UP.

Sykes, P.J., Meason, I. and Woods, P. (1985) *Teacher Careers, Crises and Continuities*. London: Falmer P.

Tate, A. (1964) What is creative writing? *Wisconsin Studies in Contemporary Literature* 5 (3), 181–184.

Tatum, S. (1993) 'The Thing Not Named': The end of creative writing in the English department', *ADE Bulletin* 106 (Winter), 30–34 <http://web2.ade.org/ade/bulletin/n106/106030.htm>. Accessed 19 September 2010.

Thompson, C. (2009) Clive Thompson on the new literacy. *Wired Magazine* 17.09 <http://www.wired.com/techbiz/people/magazine/17-09/st_thompson>. Accessed 02 January 2011.

Tolstoy, L. (1986) The death of Ivan Illych. In R. Bausch and R.V. Cassill (eds) *The Norton Anthology of Short Fiction* (7th edn) (pp. 1452–1491). New York: W.W. Norton & Co.

Tobin, L. (1991) Reading students, reading ourselves: Revising the teacher's role in the writing class. *College English* 53 (Mar.), 333–348.

Tobin, L. (2004) *Reading Student Writing: Confessions, Meditations, and Rants*. Portsmouth: Boynton/Cook.

Tompkins, J. (1980) The reader in history: The changing shape of literary response. In J. Tompkins *Reader-Response Criticism: From Formalism to Post-Structuralism* (pp. 201–223). Baltimore: Johns Hopkins UP.

Trimbur, J. (1989) Consensus and difference in collaborative learning. *College English* 51 (6), 602–616.

Tyler, K. (2007) The tethered generation. *HR Magazine* 53: (May) <http://www.shrm.org/hrmagazine/articles/0507/0507cover.asp>. Accessed 12 August 2010.

Vandenberg, P. (2004) Integrated writing programmes in American universities: Whither creative writing? *New Writing: An International Journal for the Practice and Theory of Creative Writing* 1 (1), 6–13.

Vanderslice, S. (2006) Workshopping. In G. Harper (ed.) *Teaching Creative Writing* (pp. 147–157). London: Continuum.

Vanderslice, S. (2010) Once More to the Workshop: A Myth Caught in Time. In D. Donnelly (ed.) *Does the Writing Workshop Still Work?* (pp. 30–35). Bristol: Multilingual Matters.

Wandor, M. (2008) *The Author is not Dead, Merely Somewhere Else*. Houndmills: Palgrave.

Weiss, T. (1989) A personal view: Poetry, pedagogy, per-versities. In B. Siegel *The Writer in the University* (pp. 149–176). Newark: U of Delaware P.

Welch, N. (1996) Revising a writer's identity: Reading and 'Re-Modeling' in a composition class. *CCC* 47 (1), 41–61.

Wilbers, S. (1980) *The Iowa Writers' Workshop: Origins, Emergence, & Growth*. Iowa City: U of Iowa P.

* Note: Website links to AWP need a member login.

For Product Safety Concerns and Information please contact our EU Authorised Representative:

Easy Access System Europe

Mustamäe tee 50

10621 Tallinn

Estonia

gpsr.requests@easproject.com